WHY I FAIL

FOREWORD BY

Prof. Abdullahi Y. Shehu

Ph.D, OON, FCIN

Former Director General of GIABA

WHY I FAIL

Comrade Fayiah LEIBA

WHY I FAIL

Acknowledgements

Let me humbly seize this opportunity to register sincere gratitude to people who made an impact in my personal life.

I salute you for nurturing my career these past years and steering me down the road that led to this book, I owe many thanks to Rose, my dear wife – without whom I would have never known the true meaning behind an adage: *"Behind every successful man, there is a GREAT Woman."* My sons, for your sake, I have to be very rich in order for me to help make a paved lane for you to achieve the best results in life. My special thanks to three female colleagues that I called MPS for making this book deal happen and keeping it on track during a very tight and hectic time. I would like to thank the editing team(s) for helping me put my story on the page.

Some of you saw the potential in me and suggested to me to write this book and making it a reality, I would like to thank everyone at Graceworx Publishers, South Africa.

For bringing this book home to Sierra Leone and making sure it is published with the utmost care, I would like to thank everyone at Graceworx Publishers, South Africa.

For reading this manuscript in its early stages and sharing thoughts and ideas to make it the finished product you hold in your hands, I owe my deepest gratitude to group: Ecrivain du Royaume and the Bethel Church in Dieuppeul III for spurring the incarcerated dream in me to come out and fly free.

And, finally, to my mother, Tewa Satta LEIBA, for bringing me into this world and making me the man I am today, I owe the greatest debt, a debt I can never repay. Just a lesson that I cannot conclude without sharing with others: *"Don't listen to my advice and do not do anything about it. Make use of it, lest another seize the opportunity and prosper with the advice you once ignored".* To date, I am with that mindset, Mama.

TABLE OF

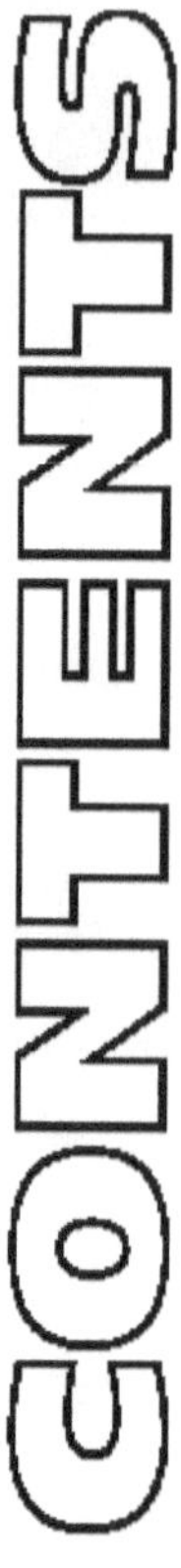

This is the message I want to put across

It's actually not a failure, it's rather a success metaphor shown in a negative form or turning the negative situation(s) into a success bid or still the hard lessons learnt in the course of time and the methods used to achieve good or better results.

See this message here. There is a clever saying that says *Experience is the best teacher.* This might be true to some extent. However, a wise man once said that though experience is the best teacher. It's better if it is not your own experience.

'Long ago, I realized that success leaves clues, and that people who produce outstanding results do specific things to create those results. I believed that if I precisely duplicated the actions of others, I could reproduce the same quality of results that they had." – Tony Robbins
There are certain mistakes you make in life that may put you in a space where it is impossible to pick any

lessons from them. In other words, the experience of another is the best Teacher.

That's why I thought of writing this book in the first place in order for it to be reference book for many of our young adults. So that they do not commit the same errors like what I did.

In August 2014, a friend of mine tagged me on Facebook with a link entitled Rich Dad monopoly game. I clicked of course to see what was in for me; behold, I discovered an information gold mine, which I exploited and have benefitted from that single click that day to date.

FOREWORD

I take great pleasure in writing the Foreword for this scintillating book – "Why I Fail" – for obvious reasons. First, I have known Comrade for over a decade and I was mesmerized by his conception and presentation of life issues in a metaphorical context in the book; secondly, the book speaks exactly what Comrade is in terms of world view, critical thinking and imaginative thought; thirdly, his in-depth inspiration from the spiritual lessons he has drawn from the Holy Bible and his narrative of environmental influence on his world view and experiences; and most importantly, his frank narration of his personal experiences, which some may appear too private to be shared with unknown persons, but the lessons are indelible for building a life style of value.

"Why I Fail" is indeed a great lesson of life. The message in it is presented in a metaphorical logic of successes because of failures – as the saying goes – you cannot succeed without trials and failures. That is why in my view, the 'Fail' is written in present, rather than past tense 'Failed'. This is highly innovative and thoughtful. The preliminary chapters of the book contain important lessons, especially for the youth who aspire to succeed in their life endeavours. One would agree entirely with Comrade that 'experience is the best teacher but the experience of another is the best teacher' for human development. This is why he wrote the book for others to learn from his own mistakes.

There are many lessons of life in the book, but suffice it to mention just a few. The first is that "sometimes you can be punished for doing what is right". Indeed, I recall an instance when he suffered this when I was the Director General of GIABA where he is a staff member. I cannot give details of that here but I believe he retained the memory and he learned from that lesson. The second important message Comrade conveyed in this book is that 'you should not engage in any battle that would not yield any positive result. This is a strategic lesson for future leaders indeed. Again, he opined that not all opportunities are to be taken; sometimes opportunities could be traps for you to fail. And finally, he admonished his readers not to attempt to destroy others because your devilish plans may boomerang against you. It is because he has broken the rules in these lessons that motivated him to write this book. Great lessons indeed!

I agree with the author that "the content (of the book) is full of success messages and the way forward on how to remain on track when things aren't in your favour' (p.13). He therefore captures the relevance of strategic partnership as an important ingredient for success; and admonishes on how to manage failures and turn them into successes. He believes that everyone is the architect of one's self as he puts it metaphorically that "the Enemy of My Enemy is Myself". Perhaps the greatest key to success as characterized in the book is FOCUS: 'Following One's Course Until Success'.

Finally, I must commend the author for his creativity and imagination relayed for others to learn from his experiences. I also commend the quality of the book and recommend it for students and the youth in general who need to draw inspiration from the lessons in this book to overcome the challenges of modern technology and globalization.

Professor Abdullahi Y. Shehu, *Ph.D, OON, FCN*

Former Director General of GIABA.

Introduction:

The rule of three (3):

There is something very special with the figure three (3). It can be Father Abraham's three days' vo3yage to the mountain to sacrifice his son, Isaac. It can also be Jesus's death and his resurrection on the third day.

No, in this context I am talking about the three lessons everyone can learn in order to avoid many troubles we go through in life. Sometimes there is no need to fight back, but you have that inner VOICE. It can be very soft but in any case POWERFUL. Listen to it, though by weighing the consequences. If it is not worth the battle — run for safety like what Joseph did when Potiphar's wife wanted to sleep with him because he was a very purposeful young man with a great future ahead of him. So, he ran in order to save his image but unfortunately it turned out that the safety he was running for landed him into prison.

Tough lessons come in various forms; sometimes you can be punished for doing what is RIGHT. Relax, it can happen — never say "if I had known I would not have done that good thing and then getting punished for seeking to do well. Other people have experienced that and the only thing I can tell you is to take courage and move on with life. It is not the end and never will it be your final destiny.

Now the three (3) rules to live by.

There was a very good story that strokes the cords of my personal life, which I saw myself in it so clearly; "One upon a time"– as we were taught in our respective schools and the story begins.

The giant dog and flying eagle near a steep river bank where the eagle sat at the steep river bank motionless to hunt for its prey which is basically the fish in the river. The dog went closer towards the eagle but noticed that the eagle was not minding it; the dog got irritated and wanted to show the eagle its might by grabbing it and killing it.

Rule one. Sometimes the best response to provocation is to not get into a fight. If you do, when you don't have the supporting facts in place, you may be doing it to your own disadvantage. The dog leaped to catch the eagle that was nestled higher above on the steep river bank You can guess what will happen even if the dog catches the eagle, the angle to which it has leaped to get the eagle — if at all, it is going to land and it will fall straight away and land in the river instead of the bank of the river. Though the dog can swim, but once in that river with prey it will be compelled to release it because it will now be forced to fight rather to get back to the safer river bank. So, that effort to engage in any battle that will not yield results is not necessary.

Rule two: *Not all opportunities are to be taken. Some are just traps.* In West Africa for instance, there is this tendency where the section of the Mediterranean Sea linking Europe and Africa has become the next graveyard for young and purpose-driven West African youth who are in constant battle to try and cross to Europe in search of greener pastures. Sometimes they actually get there, it is only very few of them actually able to make the crossing I mean; only a small number of them survive this risk. To be frank with you, I had that same mindset before, but that mindset was wiped away in 2004 through an overseas further education orientation program organized in Dakar, Senegal for aspiring youth who want to further their education in the West. Since that day I changed my mind and refocused my attention into making myself better in Africa instead. It has shown to me that it is just the mindset that required being with checks and balances.

Rule three: *Sometimes a person becomes so determined to destroy another person that they end up destroying themselves.* This is a watchful moment for every one of us in our respective lives. We are always constantly stepping on toes of other people in our environments. It is normal. Let's consider this for a moment — the relationship between the teeth and the tongue. Mistakenly, the teeth can bite the tongue and it hurts a lot, but nobody has gone to the hospital to remove the teeth because of a few bites the tongue has suffered from it.

With these three (3) rules in mind you ought to be very smart in your dealings with your neighbor. On a personal level, I have broken all the rules, which served as a recipe of *"Why I Fail"* in most instances but I did dust myself and woke up when I fell and today, I can share with the younger generation not to repeat the same errors.

This title came to mind one morning while I was driving to drop my son, Ebenezer to school and then continue to work

I was listening to an audio book called: Rich Dad Poor Dad.

In it, Rich Dad's son (Robert T. Kiyosaki) was in Singapore and one of the best female journalists was there to interview him. She was not happy about her job; she had wanted to be a bestselling writer.

Rich Dad, in the person of Robert T. Kiyosaki corrected her by saying: *"I'm not a writer, but an author instead".* This correction didn't go down well with her personally. He went on saying, he was a C grade student and had failed English, but today, he is one of the bestselling authors of our time. The female journalist felt humiliated, but he was saying the reality. For any book to make its mark, it has to be seen in its title for anyone to ask or want to see why that title.

Before I could get to my office BACOCO that day I have figured out already the success story I was writing must have a metaphor (success disguised in a form of a failure from a distance.) I actually didn't fail but I nearly did if I was not quick to act promptly.

The content is full of success messages and the way forward on how to remain on track when things aren't in your favor.

Remember this, King David, after he killed Goliath, he became famous for a time. All of the sudden, things changed for him in a negative manner. Thereafter, He ran to save his life. To a point, when even those from his household were against him. Imagine yourself in such a scenario. It's very tough, you know.

Again, this is it: Why I Fail. I hope, after having read it, you will no longer think that it can't happen to you. But when it happened, you now know how to get out it safe and sound.

God bless you.

Chapter | One

Strategic Partnership

No one is an island and no man stands alone

***** John Donne *****

One of my sons, Ebenezer has two close classmates as his lovely friends. In fact, they invite each other home in fact Ebenezer has gotten the authorization to invite his friends to our home. Due to their friendship, Ebenezer wants to school in France in order to continue to be with his friends. The reason being, Baptiste is originally from France, while Simon is from one of South American countries but his parents moved to France in August 2018 to continue their lives there. Hence, France is the order of the day in the life of Ebenezer after his high school studies in Dakar, even though he has to go through elementary schooling before. They are his strategic partners. Will that dream come to pass? It is a question that is well posed, but the answer is with the Lord God.

Whenever we speak of strategic partnership, the first thing that crossed our minds is this: He is talking business issues here. In fact, life in itself is business oriented. I have heard a lot of people say things like this: *Money does not create happiness.* Yes! However, without it, life can be very miserable and you are now learning that hard truth.

The one that coached some of us into how to write a book, during one of his interactions with us one evening when we were discussing issues related to money, said:

"See brethren. When you are poor, you are nobody, so it is better to endeavor to be rich financially than poverty. King Solomon in the Bible, do you know why he requested wisdom from the Lord God? Because his father King David left him with a lot of heritance, hence he needed wisdom on how to handle the riches left in his care." - Etienne Katanku Fortunatus

His sharing was backed by this biblical verse: So I said, *"Wisdom is better than strength." But the poor man's wisdom is despised, and his words are no longer heeded.* Ecclesiastes 9:16 | NIV

There are certain areas or environments in each and every one of us; you will never be allowed to go there if you are very poor. This is why coaches charge huge amount of money for their coaching services particularly in coaching concerning riches, because if they are poor and then they are coaching you and me to be rich. It will not sit well with us; we will not see the authority behind what they are saying.

This drew my attention to one of these football players whose name was added into one of these French dictionaries: Le Robert that welcomes in his 2016 edition two words coming straight from football: thus, alongside the newcomers "degun", "sjaller" or "pad Thai", we find the verb "zlataner" (in reference to the Swedish player: Zlatan Ibrahimovic) and the common name 'Routourne", dear to Franck Ribéry.May 20, 2016. The zlatanate means to win a football match or act in a way to dominate your opponent. Seriously speaking, this guy does not respect his coaches because he is paid more than them, hence the coach rather align with his own point of view if he wants him to perform well.

Therefore, since such a great cloud of witnesses surrounds us, let us throw off everything that hinders and the sin that so easily entangles and let us run with perseverance the race marked out for us. Hebrews 12:1 | NIV

On Sunday 17th June 2018, after having taken my lunch which my beautiful wife, Rose has prepared after we came from church service. I decided to go get some sleep as soon as I woke up I drew near my iPhone in order to check the time, while I was watching the time, a tweet from Elon Musk emerged and caught my attention.

The enemy of my enemy is myself. – Elon Musk

First, I ignored and went on to ease myself and moved to the kitchen to get room temperature water to drink While I was drinking the water, I again crosschecked the tweet: *"The enemy of my enemy is myself."*

Then, I opened the Twitter app in order to see other comments on this single tweet. One of the comments caught my attention as well. Most often on social media, we spend a huge amount of time debating sometimes unnecessary things to prove our points or stance or sometimes, believes which we have no idea whether the person on the other side of the planet knows in fact, what we are talking about. Before we realized it, the appointment time we have been waiting for has gone past us, we are late. If only we could refrain from that foolish argument and move on.

Strategic partnership is a decision you have to make for yourself for it to prosper lest it will just be an ordinary decision with no tangible results. Some distractions are actually not worth the effort like Elon Musk rightly put that the enemy of my enemy is myself. If you avoid or ignore those stupid comments on any social media and channeled that precious time to something beneficial, the gain will be wonderful.

This will help us not to fail in our mind; I have observed that anything anyone has mastered very well must have cost a lot of time and commitment to that goal. Where others may now see and marvel at what the person has accomplished

This is not just for the heroes of the faith, but in secular life as well. When you are tempted on your faith in your mind, don't fail. God can do the impossible, if only you keep your mind from negative thoughts of failure. People might have told you that you are a good for nothing person or you not qualified for such and such task, just remember the story of David and Goliath. Giants may be big but your God is bigger and in fact a strategic partner always. Also remember the story of the woman in the Bible with the bleeding issue for 12 solid years.

Just when she thought it was permanent, then the strategic partner (Jesus) stepped in to grant her the required healing.

Every other voice will be negative on you but never lose hope for God is working behind the scenes unknown to you and to your enemies in fact, he is our strategic partner.

When you are succeeding, you don't need confidence but when things are going wrong or not your way, you need a lot of little courageous steps, which will then turn into a serious confidence to keep you moving on.

Technically, nothing is different, but something is different. Are you complaining about things, that your ancestors would have dreamt of having? But never laid an eye on them let alone owning them? They dreamed about what we are enjoying today and yet complained about the quality of the service of that thing, your great grandparents must have dreamt about and yet, did not even see – you have it.

They didn't have freedom but they sang redemption songs anyway. They handed you the baton, so make sure you go further. We are the generation under the new covenant called grace. It is easy to let light afflictions affect us.

Compared to our ancestors, what we might be complaining about today, are the comforts they dreamed about and could not lay their naked eyes on let alone owning them.

Your relatives suffered greatly for you to be where you are today. None of us got to where we are today on our own, but somebody made that sacrifice for you to be where you are today.

I am where I am now because my parents kept God's place intact in their lives. They withstood hardships.

The people of Israel made it to the Promised Land on foot. Today, we do so via transport systems such as vehicles, trains, ships, and airplanes, yet we complain about the low quality service.

Heroes of faith are not just people in the Bible. Your actions maybe actions of heroes … you need to be a strategic partner for the next generation to follow like what we are currently following.

Have models to follow

"Long ago, I realized that success leaves clues and that people who produce outstanding results do specific things to create those results. I believed that if I precisely duplicated the actions of others, I could reproduce the same quality of results that they had."

***** Tony Robbins *****

Following models can mean different things to various people. If your partner in a group has a different philosophy, you may have a great idea, but it will not be easily sold to them.

When people refused to support with newly impregnated idea, which requires enough care on the initial stage, it will be difficult to survive the test of time.

Whenever you receive a favor, it is because of a favor connection. On one Thursday morning, while we were heading to school first and then, my office (BACOCO), my car refused to start and I called the mechanic, but little did I know that the car couldn't be repaired for an interval of 10 days. All of a sudden, I got my favor connection with one of my colleague's taxi chauffeur who picks her daughter from school and drops her home to assist me that day because I will not be able to pick my son, Ebenezer. I got an immediate OK response from the taxi driver that kept me wondering, until this day. Two weeks later I was opportune to listen to Pastor Joel Osteen's Sermon: *Favor Connection*. The sermon which drew my attention to the above mentioned event is what I am now bringing to your attention.

Favor Connection can also be seen as a strategic partnership. Noah found favor with the Lord, his life and the lives of his entire family were spared and God established His covenant with him and this covenant went down to the notice of every one of us today. They were connected to the favor and their lives were spared.

Because of the strategic partnership association, favor connection can be established and can be either beneficial or negative depending on which type of favor connection you have engaged yourself into.

The more blessed your favor connection is established with blessed people, the more blessed you will be. The question I want to pose to you: What are you connected to?

Find some good favor connections, you are going to become just like them. If you have an eagle mind-set and choose to hang around with chickens then expect your destiny to be an eagle type destiny; No! Never, people are exposing themselves to higher levels that they have never experienced before. If they courageously stick to that state of mind, sooner or later they will experience a positive life in their personal life. Their individual vision would be expanded.

"When God put you with eagles don't have a chicken mentality" – Joel Osteen. Every one of us knows that most of the problems we are faced with in life are basically from the connection we established with people (our environment) also known as the soil or Friend's we have in our lives.

So get yourself prepared if you live with a limited vision, you will never go where you can't accept in your mind. In fact, this brought in serious thought for me about five years after meeting with my now wife, Rose. She had a challenge to do away with bad or poor relationship that I observed with some of her friends, some were good but few were not fit for purpose. She told me that she can't get away from friends she grew up with since her childhood because of a man she just met. I responded in return that you cannot continue to be their best friend like before and expect me to be your husband. If I have spent my life with many friends but at a certain point, I have to give up that friendship and forge ahead because I wanted to develop and have discovered that I have become the smartest man in the group, which showed me my group was too small for me to continue with them.

In the Scripture, Naomi and Ruth were both widows. Naomi saw a man named Boaz, she respected the favor experienced in the life of Boaz Hence, she guided her widow daughter in law to get closer to this special man, Boaz She connected with someone with favor. – Ruth 2:22 | NIV

You respect that favored person. She could have dismissed the proposal of her mother-in-law but she took it to heart and acted accordingly. She recognized that Boaz was an eagle on whose wing she can soar with no fear.

Are there favor connections in your life?

That favor is going to rub off on you, what you sow into that favor connection is actually what you are going to reap. If you sow into gossip connection, you are obviously going to reap that in return.

People are expanding their businesses because they have sown into favor expansion connection. We all have our friends but please let's endeavor that those friends are favor connected ones to catapult us to higher levels into our respective businesses.

To reach the next level of favor connection; you need to have a habit of celebrating those who are celebrating their breakthroughs. If you cannot celebrate other people success, you will never get there or pass them.

If we humbled ourselves what you are connected to will eventually come back to you. You need to sow into where you want to go. There is no success into your life that comes by accident.

Someone is more blessed than us; we should never be or get discouraged for their success. The favor in their lives is an indication of your next level blessings.

If you are connected with people with favor, it will flow on you. If you find yourself with people with connected favor there are several prominent people in your local area that you can seek to get connected with in fact, they will be glad if they notice that you are in their lives to bless them and not to harm them. They too will do likewise. I say this in humility, 20 years ago, I had a family friend who was older than me. I tried to keep the relationship healthy, I have gotten further in life than him but we have kept our friendship on a level playing field stage.

We don't have to compete with people, there is a place where they inspired you to become a better person. Trying to make them look bad is a serious waste of time. If you sow disrespect, you are going to reap disrespect.

Somebody God puts into your life. Let us become the kind of people who celebrate the breakthrough of others, you see that Elisha recognized the favor of Elijah. What you sow into, is what you are going to reap later in life.

Elisha just kept on honoring. Fortunately for him, he received a double portion of what he was expecting. God will surely double what you are expecting if you celebrate the connected favor of others cheerfully.

Many pastors sow into the ministries of other very important pastors. Sometimes, I asked myself this question: why do they cater more for these men that already have plenty?   This is a spiritual principle. Look around, find the people that God has blessed and be a blessing to them. We ought to recognize the favor connection.

Are you connected to anyone that has what you want? The answer is in your own hands. Get yourself on the look out of favor connected strategic partnership.

Chapter Two

Managing failures

Failure is very good but it has to be properly managed lest, we will not learn any lesson from them. I am going to mention five solid failures so that tomorrow whenever you sense something similar; you can avoid it through the few how to lessons I have learnt from them or through them.

I will be starting with my own story, which may serve

as a catalyst for someone or my young sons not to ever repeat such mistakes in their lives. March 1997, I bumped into a supposed lonely mother with a 1 and ½ years old daughter. After having shared her plight with me, I blindly trusted her with my life.

Failure 1: I am a follow talk person, which has presented me with mitigated results – the good and the bad ones alike.

In 1999, my mom came to visit where we were staying. She actually came for a month but she could barely spend that period with us. She packed her things and left, however before she left she told me:

'My son, this family you have chosen a wife into is not a family that is considered average people like us. Talk –less considering you are a husband". I replied 'Maman! I didn't meet this one richly. She was in fact, struggling and I came to her aid and so she cannot tell me anything tomorrow that she took care of me. 'Her response was 'Mark my words. She will never respect or be submitted to you as your wife. "

So, she left for Koundou Lengo Bengou. Every blessed day, our home was a battlefield and we were fighting and seeing this situation, she told me that she will never be part of our marriage.   Never! Ever! Truly folks, she did just that.

I spent 10 years in a hectic fiancée mode and 9 other years in a legally matrimonial, hectic one, which got me thinking it will one day work I wanted to make a difference in her life, but to no avail. It is then, and there I knew, if someone wants to be great, it is easy to be, but if they are not willing to be or don't want to be, DON'T waste your time and effort. It will never work

How did I manage my failures in a failed marriage?

It was tough but worth the experience. When I knew or truly suspected that I was into failed marriage in 2008 after the birth of my first son, Ebenezer, I chose to have protected sexual intercourse because I never wanted to have any other child with this unscrupulous wife. On 31st December 2013, my New Year Resolution was to stop requesting any sexual intercourse with her until we are pronounced divorced.

It was very tough initially but it was doable. You can give it a try if you find yourself in a situation that will require a strong discipline from your part.

In addition to the above-mentioned scene, I decided to leave her alone and provided her with all the freedom to do whatever she wants to my own detriment. The freedom was so much to a point, whenever I give instructions to be carried out, she will provide counter instructions and it was her own instructions that will be respected and I will pay for any danger her counter instructions led to.

The home became a war zone, with two factions:
- ✓ The mother faction; and
- ✓ The daddy faction.

The scene was well demarcated into two partial sizes. The mother with her daughters and the daddy with his son, at least a soul to be saved later on. The law as we all know is never fair in the life on earth. It took that persistent widow a huge amount of time to get the justice she has ever fought for. I managed my failures to pay for child support, and yet kept the son I am paying support for, because I wanted him to become someone important in the society.

Sometimes, your options will push you to extra mile efforts

This is Wednesday 15th August 2018 it was a public holiday in Senegal, my duty station since 2006. I was at home with my very sweet family members listening to my long list of business-oriented audiobooks. However, the trash bag was giving some alarming and very bad odors. My wife, Rose in her exactly, 6th month old pregnancy requested that I take out this smelling trash to the trash collector truck because the odor was unbearable for any expecting mother.

I took the trash bag as I was going down the staircases; she was as well spraying my expensive Oriflamme perfume behind me in order not to let the bad odor disturb the neighbors.

I drove to the area, as soon as I climbed the junction where the Brioche d'Oree bakery shop is situated; I spotted two of these trash trucks coming in my direction. I stopped there to see where they were heading to, one of them took my right hand side, which was in fact heading in our area, whilst the other, took the left hand side of the Peugeot 407 that I was driving. I am a left-handed man, so I chose to follow the vehicle on my left hand side. To me, I thought it will soon stop and I will as well stop by and take off this dirt from my car and then turn around and head home.

However, to my greatest surprise I was in for a long hurl. I was now obliged to chase the trash vehicle for a distance of two kilometers, which was actually not funny. I had never expected such a marathon that early morning. I had no choice but to cover that distance in order to get the dirt off my car. Anywhere, it stops; I will do the dumping of the dirt and turn to go back home. Then, I quickly realized that I have made a wrong choice, but I have no other solution, but to persevere the strain until this said vehicle reached its stopping point, which I later saw to be a bushy area. The truck stopped and I also parked just behind it and got off my car, picked smelling dirt in the boot and throw it in the trash truck and turned around and left the environment.

As soon as I arrived my wife, said "You took a bit long" I responded." Yes, I went through a marathon due to bad choice I have made" It has served me as one of these life lessons, which I will name, Sometimes, one of your options will push you to go the extra mile in discharging any of your duty services.

Putting the cart before the horse

A wife of my friend introduced me into a business that I have been avoiding for ages. In fact, through my plenty audiobooks listening, I have come to understand, in order for you to make a headway in life, you ought to know how to sell. However, it has been that I have been avoiding almost all throughout my life, which is even something that has made yet to be an average individual when I should have been my own self-made boss.

First, I told her, I will buy the items for my wife. She accepted and told me, it is a choice. You can now choose to be a user and if it makes meaning to you, you can then move from just an ordinary user, to a seller, you can now become a builder. The company name is Oriflamme, a Swedish based company, which is into cosmetic products based on organic materials.

I have been guided a few times, and the trend is moving very slowly, because I am still trying to avoid been a seller, in the first place.

In the process I have thus far introduced the product to a few of my contacts across the sub Saharan region, Africa as a whole. A family friend wrote back to tell me that he/she had established a Non-Governmental Organization (NGO) which is something, he has to commit most of his time to. He thought that the business I had of the products and program is very much interesting but he indicated that he was not into getting himself involved for now.

In plain words, he was directly telling me. "Go look elsewhere for people interested in doing business with you, but as for me, I am into NGO work instead".

This was our WhatsApp chatting messages between Manenda Franco (MF) and Comrade Fayiah LEIBA (Me). The chats went something like this, and I will roughly quote:

> **Manenda Franco**: *Hi! Thanks very much for sharing the idea with me. However, I can't be part of it, because, beside my work, I've opened an organization that has the potential to grow rapidly. It will make me to be an employer. So, apart from my job that has taken my time, NGO also needs my time.*

> **Comrade**: *I then asked him, "is the Organization an NGO?"*

> **Manenda Franco**: *He responded by saying: Yes sir. Local NGO working for disable individuals.*

Comrade: *I am asked the financial aspect: "Hmmm. Where will finances come from, if I may ask?"*

Manenda Franco: *He responded: "we get funding from donor funding and fund raising activities. After two years, I will be legible to apply for big funding. For now, we are only getting small funding to implement short-lived projects.*

We also get funding from the government. We have implemented some projects already.

We will be completing one of the projects next week and we will report on it.

Comrade: *I asked him this question: "For how long will you be begging to fund this Organization?"*

To the above mentioned question, he responded lengthily and even defended his stance that he is not the only one that has been begging for funds, but other organizations as well. It did not start with him.

Manenda Franco: *There are several organizations globally that depends on fund raising. So, I'm not the only one. Besides, when one applies for projects, you will be asked about your own source of income. Our fund raising has a specific target.*

We used to use our money. Now, the fund raising is helping us a lot and people are contributing because they believe in us. I prefer it (my NGO) to this one (business). I can see how my idea helps the vulnerable in society. If I get big funding, I will create jobs for the jobless. God will help me.

Comrade: *My brother, have you considered the day you get retired and no longer on your feet to work or look out for fundraising programs? Think well.*

Manenda Franco: *We have to organize several events that can raise funds for us. We will also use the money for its intended purposes.*

I will not be raising funds forever. It's all about planning for my future. By the grace of God, when I get old, I should rely on my savings, end of service benefit and a good pension from

NASSIT. After that, my family will have a little business to keep life going. I have a good plan for my old age sir.

Comrade: *Let me again ask this:*

Is the Organization in your name, please?

Or, it was created by you and you now co-opted people to work with you?

Manenda Franco: *I created the organization with a Friend. I am the head and I am the principal signatory to the account. Nobody will fight me for it.*

Comrade: *Then, you are fine. Thanks for the kind gesture & many blessings in all your God-driven endeavors, amen.*

Manenda Franco: *Amen. Stay blessed.*
That ended our conversation.

Why am I bringing this to anyone who wants to listen or read this?

If you have look through history many foundations that

have been established, be it in Africa or elsewhere around the globe. It all started from a business idea. Once the business is well established and it grows into something independent and now has sufficient financial resources. Then the time to give it back to the either nearby community is a relief program for disaster-stricken areas or something like that. However, if you have established an NGO and start to look for financial resources to carry out the activities of the established NGO, it is going to be very difficult. This is why I call it "putting the cart before the horse. As we know the horse will not be able to move within such scheme of things, African brethren, let's start-thinking entrepreneurship instead of NGOs.

"Success for many of us comes in different forms. Not everyone succeeds in one way, but the other person may not." - Clayton Geoffreys. This was shown in this unauthorized biography of John Stockton. I salute the author for a job well done.

There is no formulae or road maps for success in general.

Those considered great have a title. Stockton's own success was not with title, but the author rightly put it and you cannot never see it and fail to notice it.

In fact, it reminded me of the story of Jonathan and King David in the Bible, King Saul's son. He was supposed to be the one enthroned as king after his dad, but chose to give up that right for David instead.

This is what was displayed in Stockton's story as shown by the author, Clayton Geoffreys because he used to supply balls for his teammates to score. A selfless act that made me to love the book and can recommend it, you want to be selfless please choose to read this story.

This is how the author of John Stockton's story, displayed the basketball player.

Championships define the players' careers. A talented shooting cannot win you a title. He was there to fill in the place of others. – Clayton Geoffreys

He always fought for his friends to score.

To every disadvantage, there are opportunities.

It is early morning, my wife Rose asked me to go to the rooftop and spread our clothes to dry. The morning was pleasant because the sky was cloudy and the heat was mild.

As soon as I saw that the spot where birds used to come and spend the night was now disserted and one can no longer find excrements all over the place. At first, I was shocked at seeing that place was now cleaned with no excrements of the birds.

Then I quickly started processing or analyzing the reason this place we usually have to clean. I remembered that the birds have always been here. Since the beginning of July 2018 to date (11th August 2018) when I was penning down this information, there was water shortage in our area. So, we left the 10-litre Kombra bottles at the rooftop the entire time. Tap water will resume running full time like it has always been the case and we can then refill them.

Nobody likes a noisy environment. These empty bottles cannot stand-alone because the breeze is always moving them around and they have made the rooftop very noisy and no longer conducive for these birds to come around and spend the night as usual.

A friend once told one of his colleagues that if ever she was to improve in her career, it could never happen in a peaceful environment or without enemies. See.

Whenever you have enemies in your daily routine of life activities, it is because you are either a star or a hardworking person. So, never concentrate your energy on the distraction in your midst, but rather focus your attention on what you are doing to the point of success.

Can marriage succeed without love?

It depends and no two people can maintain a marriage, but one.

Many of us are going through serious comfort-related difficulties which we have become accustomed to and they are no longer seen as a challenge in our midst.

Sometimes, we think we are not comfortable with person A, only to go and discover later the characteristics of person A are better than what you would have found outside.

I am opportune to be a host to one of my sisters-in-law. Her stay with us was very much awesome, because she ate what we eat and life was very okay from that stand point because we were comfortable with that she was also comfortable with it.

In my casual one on one discussion with her on one of

these evenings after our family devotion; she started commending me for the way I am handling her junior sister. This is what every young lady today across the whole world is looking for. For you to have a husband that loves you. She continued, I have everything one can imagine in marital home but there is one thing that is lacking and that is: LOVE. She paused to control her emotions, lest she cries. 'For over 24 years, I have never ever experienced love in a single day from my husband", she said.

Well Comrade Fayiah LEBA often has a quick solution to every problem. Even though sometimes, the proposed solutions are not feasible solutions. Yet, I told her maybe it is because when he was growing up in his then family with his parents he never experienced love. You can only give what you have, not what you don't have to another. Particularly if he is a busy person and may not have time to learn new skills – such as how to make love to his wife for instance. Maybe, if he retired, he might likely learn to love you. However, he may have certain good characteristics that I may not have too. So I told her 'In life, you cannot have everything, my dear sister-in-law. Let us continue to pray for him, he might one day change the stiffness and start loving you for he is actually depriving you what he is supposed to give you."

On the other side of the two faces of a coin, the junior sister, who happens to be my wife does not like someone that is so loving and attentive to her too much. A scene of one's craving is another's disgusted act.

Fishing has its own seasons and times.

At the start of every month or at just after New month begins, I visit the seashore to get my fish provision for that ongoing month. I have been doing this for the past 10 years, but never knew that there were seasons where you have a lot of catch and there were seasons, where there is scarcity in fish provision.

So, this fine Thursday morning early morning I woke up and we went through devotion and waved goodbye to my beautiful wife and got into the car and put on my audio-book entitled: The 100 best selected books by Jack Covert and TODD SATTERSTEN I then moved to Yara Carpa beach, the seashore.

Once there, I got the shock of my life! We could not catch any fish. I combed through sails moving from ups and down and I could not spot good fish for our home. Then, I decided to get from fish hawkers, whom by their behavior you know that you will not be doing yourself any favor because I have never been their customer and they hated me for that.

Do you know the reason? It is because of a fish worth of 1000 francs CFA they will cost it for 10,000, which will not encourage bargaining with them further, if you know the market.

There is this lady who has always been cleaning the fish for me whenever I go get the fish. Her husband is one of African immigrants that have gone to Spain by boat and is still there leaving this beautiful lady to cater for herself in the hot sun of Dakar, Senegal. Actually, she has found favor in my eyes, for every time I go buy fish; she is the one that cleans them for me.

She was the one that also disclosed to me this long history that whenever it rains, there is a scarcity in getting fish. It is when there is no rain that fish are easily caught. Strange isn't it? When I got back home and shared that with my wife, she confirmed it for me to be so.

 A child should sometimes, remain a child, and adults ought to remain adults

One early morning, while I was fetching water because

there was a shortage of water, my neighbor, Mr. Do Good came by to share his dissatisfaction with me concerning this long period of water shortage in Dakar this same period of every year.

We got into discussion concerning the above-mentioned problem.

Mr. Do Good: *This problem is becoming unbecoming my brother.*

Me: *But what can we do?*

Mr. Do Good: *This is a problem we have been encountering every year for the past decade.*

Me: *Yes, you are right. However, it looks like Dakar, which used to have 2 million people in total city population in the early 2000s mighty likely be accommodating a total population currently of between 5 to 7 million.*

With such number in view, obviously there has to be shortage somewhere either in water or other amenities. Take for instance, the housing accommodations system, which is skyrocketing every year, instead of reducing, it continues to increase making the average Senegalese's life very miserable.

Mr. Do Good: Oh my brother! That's the exact thing you have touched. Now I see why life in Dakar is gradually becoming very expensive and sometimes, we asked ourselves, why?

Me: See. SONES (Société Nationale des Eaux Sénégalaises), the Water Authority ought to give another water company the license like the only water supplier, SDE (La Senegalaise des Eaux) to operate so that when they are two, obviously – we might not experience such acute shortage any longer.

Mr. Do Good: Once there is competition, the issue of water shortage will become history and it will be over completely.

Me: Let me give you another anecdote to better make you understand what I am trying to put across. You are a Muslim, right? (Mr. Do Good responded: affirmative). Good. Whenever a Muslim man has a wife, there are always shortages in the supplies of basic amenities, such as sex, certain chores, etc. Once the second wife (co-épouse) comes in, the story changed. It's now left with the man to have a strong back to satisfy his sex ego with the two wives who will now be demanding satisfaction from his side of the contract.

Mr. Do Good: *Laughed and said, you perfectly right.*

He left me to continue to get my water. In the process, I tried to check my WhatsApp to see whether there is anything on it for me to comment on.

As soon as I opened the App, I saw that on the WhatsApp Group called Oxford Gueckedou, there were 11 unread messages, which triggered the curious me to check what is being discussed there. I observed that there were a lot of discussions and two forwarded small video clips.

A small naughty boy went and climbed on the water tank and called out 'Dad! Papa! Come! I want to commit suicide". The dad came to see the folly of his son, after having seen the scene, the dad went and brought the shovel and started digging the grave to bury his rather silly son who wanted to commit suicide.
The son saw that this was not what he was expecting.

To him, he expected the dad to apologize to him, but the dad wanted the naughty boy be buried so that the naughtiness can be done once and for all.

Happiness is contagious, and so it is the opposite.

One of these fine Sunday mornings, while we were out and about searching for where we can find water to fetch so that our Sunday cannot be in a mess.

You know Saturday nights. For young adults, they are awesome events for them because they go to nightclubs and return early the next morning to catch up on sleep. For those who were once into worldly things can easily identify themselves with this. I didn't have such leisure, because financially I'm from a poor background. It's when the belly is full you can think of amusing yourself.

We spotted a crossover Hyundai i35 vehicle filled with six youngsters – both male and females were going home with their good Wolof music playing while their windows were all rolled down so that one could hear the music so clearly.

The car was moving slowly and with frequent stops. One or two will get out and shake themselves to the rhythm of the music and get back in and move again.

They arrived at our spot, their performance drew our attention to them and we looked in amazement that so early in the morning people could be that happy, when we were struggling for water.

My wife, Rose didn't see it funny because we were looking for water and see these guys enjoying their lives. Water or no water, life must go on. They just don't care about such details.

I laughed and waved to them and they burst out in laughter because their acts have caused me to laugh and they were happy the more and got into their car and moved on with the same pace.

My wife, Rose questioned me "What is funny in their act?" In my response to her question, I just told her of the above mentioned phrase: "Happiness is contagious, and so it is the opposite"

We got our water and later left. However, sex when you are deprived of it, it does hurt a lot.

As the neighborhood ground floor tap water were filling my Kombra 10–liter bottles. Two dogs showed up; one male and then the other female, I observed the male counterpart smelling the private part of the female in order to get its dosage that good early morning and the female was as well ready for the game.

Unfortunately, the scene went on not entertained, because the male dog was castrated and the act left him with no weapon to run this important battle. The female dog positioned itself, but to no avail there were no act. The female dog roamed around in an effort to excite the male dog, nothing concrete was done. I sat there while I wait for my bottles to be filled and watched the scene and I really felt for the male castrated dog. Imagine yourself in its shoes with a beautiful lady that is every purposeful man's terrain to show up his manhood.

While getting to penetrate, you have an erectile dysfunction and cannot get it up. Would that not be the disappointment of the century?

I don't know about you but as for me, it will surely be a disappointment.

Access to any skill is the first preliminary step to personal development.

On the 19th July 2018, while I was sitting down in my parlour that fine morning when my wife, Rose who was just 4-month pregnant with our unborn son. All of the sudden, she brought me some slices of mangoes and as I was eating these slices and the same time looking through my Facebook timeline I saw that on my Facebook App; a 2-year-old baby who was swimming skill-fully in the swimming pool.

I intensely watched the video and made a comment on the clip, which read: *"Access to any skill is the first preliminary step to personal development."* This is to say, having access to any skill is the first prerequisite to any achievement of mankind on the planet, Earth.

This child learnt how to swim because they have access to the swimming pool in either their compound or within their environment. Some might say it; yes you can have access to something but neglect to learn how to exploit it. It is true partly because sometimes, having something at your disposal is one thing, making use of it is another thing altogether.

What do you have and still you have not discovered its importance in your midst?

Many a time, we have things and because we are always with them then familiarity breeds contempt or still, passive indifference sets in. Don't do that, lest you regret big time.

"Don't let them push you around even if they are pushing out of the door."

There are stages in one's life, when you have to decide what direction your personal life ought to take. Sometimes, it is very easy to implement principles in one's personal life when you are yet single. However, as soon as you choose a life partner, wherein most decisions are no longer taken by you alone but with your partner. Then there comes the tug of war in between you and your life partner because they will think that you are the only one bringing in suggestions and they have followed to the letter, maybe they feel they ought to be given a fair opportunity to either bring in their own suggestions or implement what they feel it is good even if it is not for the common good of the union.

On a personal note, I have a policy that everything I want to do has to be discussed with my soul mate (wife). I believe it is supposed to be vice versa, I should get in return what I give out in the first place. For instance, I want a friend to come and visit our family home however, before I discuss this with my friend – I am obliged by my inbuilt policy mindset, I have to first discuss with my wife. After it has been approved, then I can now present an invitation to my friend, in order for me to see if the time I want him to visit us does not conflict with his own timing. This is called an agreement corridor.

This is something I expect in return from my life partner, as well but most often, it is a serious challenge for most people. Some will do the opposite by first discussing the timing of the visit with their friend and once they have agreed upon and then come to their life partner with the result of their discussion. In any event if the timing of the visit is in conflict, let's say with the children have a school program, then confusion set in. You no longer want to postpone the friend's visit and the family members are not supposed to miss the children's program as well.

As soon as the decision is reached to choose the children's school program it is far better than the friend's visit. There is an issue at stake; stand your ground if you are right. Remember this: It's always a misunderstanding when you are on the side of RIGHT.

Chapter Three

FOCUS

I was listening to one of my audible library where I got this acronym for FOCUS: Follow One Course until Success. Not only did I get thus, but also QUIET, which is when detailed:

Question
Understand
Inspect
Empathize
Test

However, in this chapter, we are not going to talk about QUIET, but FOCUS instead. We are going to follow one course until we succeed together. If there is anything, you are going to learn from this book Let you take away this lesson that you need to follow one course until you succeed. We live in a very distracting world nowadays.

When one of my sons was born in October 2008, it

was time for me to make sure he gets the best of what I didn't get when I was his age. So, at age one, I started introducing him into computer literacy. A female colleague told me that I was not helping the boy but contributing to his downfall and requested that I stopped teaching him when he was not yet school age.

I thought I knew it all I ignored and went on to teach him the more. The boy became attached to the iPad so much if you want him to eat; the device has to be on and by his side playing before he can have appetite to eat. When he reached school age, it started becoming an issue when he got to grade 1, the first grade, where he was supposed to be doing both French and English simultaneously. The class teachers observed he lacks concentration like other pupils in class.

Both his biological mom by then and I was called by the school authority for an interview in order for the school to know where and how they can detect where lies the problem and provide their own opinion on how to help the boy to cope with the academic work

In order for him to improve his French, the school authority asked me to be speaking French to him at home, which will eventually serve as a pipeline minister to help be fluent in French so that he can verbally participate in class during French classes.

At first, he categorically refused to respond in French but I kept the FOCUS and gradually he understood I was serious with my stance and knew that I was not going to back down but he will have to submit to the new measure, and he did.

However, there was another problem, the lack of concentration in class continues, the school again stepped in to recommend an AVS (Auxiliaire de Vie Scolaire Individuel). This is a person who stands by your child in class and be telling your child to write, pay attention like other kids. This went on from CP (grade1) all the way to grade CE2 (grade 3) and when he got promoted to grade 4 this constant presence of an AVS stopped but before this time, he has made fervent promise to the stepmother, my now wife, Rose - my God-sent wife as it is stipulated in the book of Proverbs chapter 19:14 *"Houses and wealth are inherited from parents, but a prudent wife is from the Lord."*
Since then to date, Ebenezer has become a focused son, whom I am now proud of.

However before Ebenezer can become a focused child, I - the father chose to be a focused person first. I engaged myself in a divorce process which cost all my savings but I need to focus and make that huge sacrifice in order to one day share a testimony like this to the glory of the Almighty God for taking me through successfully, though very tough moments.

Usually, it is women who do request for a divorce and very rare for men to do so. In fact, my own divorce stance was very exceptional at all levels; maybe on other books I might paint the whole picture, but not here.

"What good is it for someone to gain the whole world, yet forfeit their soul?"
Mark 8:36 | NIV

I have always been negative on parents or couples that chose to work both in organizations and at the same time they want to have children, is it that easy for anyone to seize such opportunity?

It is knowing the difference between the price you will pay for such choice and the cost in terms of benefits either short term or long term ones. Some have chosen to stay home and learn petty trading, which will enable them to oversee the wellbeing of their children. While some have chosen to both work and now have to put on with their unscrupulous children whom they are not too proud of, due to what they (the parents) could not monitor and seize the opportunity to correct while it is in development stage in the lives of their children.

One amongst the two ought to choose to be a home parent while the other works to make ends meet, otherwise, you will have the money with a price That being undisciplined children to handle because the children will be left with the TV, the house help and the like.

Another disease, that is killing many younger children is sometimes caused by earlier eyesight diseases on our nowadays children. This may be because of the TV, the tablets and other dangerous electronic devices, with no proper monitoring on the children or regulated timing for the children to be exposed to them.

Many would tell you one source of income is a disaster for the family. Yes, it is quite true but there is also a catch there; money in itself, if it is not saved and invested later on – storing it will be also suicidal. In fact, it is not how much money you earned that counts but how much you can keep and invest, that counts a lot. That is why you are still poor. Yes! You heard me very well, because you don't know how to manage your financial resources.

Have you not heard; the story of an old waitress who

put her 10% of her monthly earning for close to 30 years and left that hugely accumulated compound interest amount to the charity of her community. Her local community was able to use that proceeds after her final departure from this planet to construct a university which many average people in her then community who could not afford to travel outside of their community to school, were now beneficiaries to this old waitress who knew the meaning of adage:

Little drops of water make a mighty ocean — Jakpinky

If she was able to do so, what is holding you down? Nothing! As some of you might likely want to say, but it is rather your lack of discipline. One of my high school teachers used to tell us: 'Be yourself." It is very simple, but many of us by then did struggle to be ourselves. However, if you fail to be yourself, life will compel you to be yourself. Your success will not have meaning, if your offspring cannot inherit what you have toiled for and left and they are even wishing to die earlier in order for them to sell your pieces of property and quickly share the proceeds from that. Would that not be a shame in disguise? Oh sure! So, let us invest rather in the upbringing of our children so that they can pick up the striving baton from us, lest they become our permanent dependents.

What are you spending your energy on or focusing on?

Oh how sweet to watch beautiful photos of friends on Facebook and greatly admire their beauty and sometimes, they may be showing us a false lifestyle but we tend to believe those beautiful images and start to condemn ourselves for no reason.

Didn't the Bible also advise us to rejoice with those who are rejoicing? If it so, why then do we feel discouraged when we see our friends making progress in their lives and not be happy for them and rejoice with them as well. Instead, we rather envy them or want to be like them or even want to be more than them. All right, it is good to wish good for ourselves but are we prepared to receive that goodness?

Sometimes, the life struggling situations have buffeted us so much to a point that we no longer see success as a possible thing for us as well; in fact, we talked ourselves into believing or adhering to it that it is now our natural state of lifestyle. We cannot change it.

On what do you spend your time? Many of us are

in the habit of criticism and show no tangible success to our name. We forget to know that time is not on our side whenever we engaged ourselves into doing foolish things.

This is the same criticism that made me angry with one of my former teachers, whose name I will not mention here for these reasons:

- ✓ I no longer want to make him look important; and
- ✓ Not to intrude in his privacy.

This man, when we were yet in one of these secondary schools in the early 1990s, he made some of us to trust him so much to a point where in most of these schools he taught, students saw him to be the next leader! To our disappointment, it was just a day dream for some of us.

However, one thing some of us failed to note is this; High school prestige was just a high school thing and that was all to it. Once in normal life, reality set in.

I nearly got angry with a friend when he told me: 'But that man is still an important man" This kind of pushed me to share this proverb with him: 'Kola-nut lasts long in the mouth of those who value it." For me, he was no longer important person.

Many of us spend a huge of time or focus a considerable amount of time on Facebook making comments that have never brought us any income whatsoever. It is now called the freedom of expression, which if care is not taken, is destroying many of our youth nowadays like the case of football.

Plenty talk, with no tangible achievement that anyone of us can be proud of them. However, there are some who are actually making exploits via the same vessel (Facebook). Are you focusing your efforts on tangible results that you can show tomorrow? It is a question many of us will one day ask ourselves or we are going to answer no matter what happened.

Some of us think, let's get used to this worse situation when others are thinking differently. A colleague of mine was during lunch break While waiting for lunch to be served, he was busy on his smartphone playing the Palace game (constructing a virtual palace and gaining virtual points, which will enable him to extend his palace space and improve his construction). Someone interrupted him by asking why he was so attached to the game like that?

He briefly explained to us and moved on with his game because he never wants to lose points. It didn't get me irritated but the other colleague got offended for observing that the guy was so busy with his smartphone even when the lunch was served he could not notice but went on playing his precious game.

Then, an idea came to mind in order to help him as least eat his food in a more conducive mode.

Me: *Do you know that the game you are playing is somebody else's idea that was put into a game form that you are enjoying so great like this?*

Him: *Yes, I know.*

But he still continues and never minded me.

Me: *There are three (3) people in the world:*

- ✓ *Those who make things happen;*
- ✓ *Those who use the created things; and*
- ✓ *Those who talk about them.*

It is easy to let people get us serious things that can elevate us tomorrow, through interesting programs, which are made by people like us. Elijah was a human being, even as we are. He prayed earnestly that it would not rain and it did not rain on the land for three and a half years. Yet, due to the lack of our focus on things we cannot even imagine such; talk-less of doing something that great that would have nationwide, let alone regional or international impact.

We are always limited by what we don't have and go around with a limited mentality.

Never underrate yourself.

Any time, I hear any colored person saying the Caucasians are powerful than us. It hurts me because we are created in the same image, it is rather what we think which we will become in the long run. Poverty is everywhere, so why do you consider yours more poverty stricken than the others.

Many of the great leaders in the world today never originated from rich families but from humble backgrounds and trusted their dreams wholeheartedly. They didn't come from prominent people. You can be like them provided you believe it. However, instead of trying to get even whenever someone hurts you rather borrow the heart of Joseph in the Bible. David never had social media followers, yet Samuel anointed him to be the next king. Commit today, to be an exemplary person into your family, you will be surprise on how you can become a greater person that you can ever imagine. With God's help, you can turn your humble situation into a greater person in just a matter of time.

Mbappe becomes the youngest player ever to score for France at a major finals tournament on the first 8ᵗʰ minute after the referee blew the whistle for the game to commence its 45-minute first half. The 19-year-old overtakes two French legends in becoming their youngest-ever goal scorer at a major final tournament

Kylian Mbappe has written himself into the World Cup history books with France after opening the scoring against Peru on Thursday 21st June 2018. Having drawn a blank on his tournament debut against Australia, the Paris Saint-Germain star was on hand to strike in the first half. While it appeared Olivier Giroud's deflected effort was heading into the net after fine recovery work from Paul Pogba, Mbappe made certain to put France on course for a second Group C win with a simple close-range finish and in doing so the teenage sensation set a new milestone for his nation at a major tournament.

In setting the new record, he also overtakes two Les Bleus legends. Thierry Henry and David Trezeguet were the previous holders of that distinction, achieved during the 1998 World Cup. The pair both found the net at the age of 20 as the European team lifted the trophy for the first time in their history on home soil. Mbappe, of course, does not remember that campaign and is in fact the first player born after France 1998 to score at a World Cup. Can the star teenager and his team-mates inspire France to a similar result in Russia?

On Sunday 17th June 2018, after having taken my lunch that my beautiful wife has prepared after we came from a church service. I decided to go get a nap, as soon as I woke up I checked the time on my iPhone while doing this a tweet from Elon Musk came through and caught my attention.

The enemy of my enemy is myself.

At first, I ignored and went on to the kitchen to water to drink while I was drinking the water; I again cross checked the tweet: "The enemy of my enemy is myself."

Then, I opened the Twitter App in order to see other comments on this single tweet. One of the comments caught my attention as well. Most often on social media, we spent a huge amount of time debating sometimes unnecessary things to prove our points or stance or sometimes, beliefs which we have no idea whether the person on the other side of the planet know in fact, what we talking about.

*Holiness & Glory are the clothing for our souls – by
Rev. Bignoumba Morgan (From Gabon).*

There are times in your life when you need to take
serious resolutions to either start and amend something
or move forward in your dealings. Initially, some with a
different mindset will never understand you but never
mind their stance with proper time they will understand
where you are heading to.

Before moving on, you ought to have an Action Plan.
Remember this; the Almighty God sent His only begotten
son to come and die for mankind (John 3:16). Also, if
you have observed for a period of time that your life
has been stagnant or that you are regressing instead.
The life of mankind is like someone who is riding a
bicycle, for him to move on, he has to pedal – you
either pedal and move on, or you refuse to pedal and
fall if you have both feet on the pedals.

Sometimes, we all from time to time need a retreat
period to reflect on our respective lives in general. What
is working and what is not? Great men of both our

time and in the past have done so, in order to see a bigger picture of life.

Nobody has ever, in their normal senses gone out of their home without putting on their proper dress on. This is the same with the soul or to put it in a layman's understanding, mindset. Your soul needs proper clothing, just as our bodies need the best clothing. If at all, you want to make an impact; your clothing ought to be stainless (white). Your soul needs stainless clothing, a renewed mindset.

No matter how long you have been hiding things from people, one day it can be exposed and everybody will know the kind of person you are. In fact, before God, you cannot hide anything, so why do you try to do so?

If you have a negative mindset, trust me, you will find it very difficult to improve your dealings with people within your environment.

There is this tale of the chained dog and an irritating cat. After a long while the dog owner observed it was time to release the dog from the chains in order for it to deal with this irritating cat that spent all its time, coming around to disturb the chained dog.

See what happened later on, even though the once chained dog was now released from its chains but the mindset remained on chains. Then, if the cat came to irritate, the once chained dog will chase the cat to a certain limit and stop the chase because the dog's mindset was still chained and the trouble continues.

This is how many of us have been once chained and we are now released and yet, we can no longer develop ourselves into something substantial because for some of us, our mindsets are still in chains. This is how the colonial powers came in Africa during the 17th and 18th centuries. They put boundaries between nations in Africa, changed our languages and taught us their languages, which we are today very proud of.

After they had left Africa and returned to their homelands, we still remain on those chains and in fact we are discriminating amongst ourselves. I am black and he is black – but he will tell me to go back to my country in the same Africa. Isn't this so amazing?

Most of us have lost development focus and now as neighbors we don't belong here while others are busy developing their own environments.

A problem shared, is a problem solved.

On one Saturday morning around 400am when my wife Rose woke to check if the tap was on or if there now water available for her to start the washing machine. She grudgingly stepped in the mosquito net covered bed and said "Honey, this is becoming a bit serious. This is now the 3rd day in a row that we are going without water. What is going on?"

This question woke me up and I grabbed my iPhone in order to share this concern with few people on my WhatsApp. Fortunately for me, on this App, there were two SDE water supply staff on my contact list and I typed the below message and sent it to them and waited for their response.

'Eh! My people, Do you have water at home? I mean, in your houses? Why am I asking this question? Since Monday, July 9, 2018 up until today my apartment does not have tap water running. I mean no water at all at the tap while my neighbors at the ground floor have water, when we asked their children last night when we went to get water from a family-friend house. What makes me uncomfortable, I just paid a bill of 35,000 cfa francs or even more, and I have no water. Do you find it OK for you to pay for a service and

you do not get the service?   Where are we?"

Around 7:30 am just after having gone through regular daily family devotion I got a WhatsApp call from one of my female colleagues and she made me to understand that it was a general water shortage. It was not only having that particular challenge but it was also creating other general problem. She then, advised me to get those 10-liter Kombra water bottles and go to our office and get water from there. This is because our office had a bigger water tank She further went on to advise that I should not take the matter to court.

As soon as I hanged up the call, I checked my App to see if I have received any responses, none! Around 9:30am, the landlord responded to my WhatsApp message that there is no need to go out in search of water because there is water on the ground floor. He advised me to come fetch water there and never mind the cost implications for a retired civil servant (the landlord). However, he further advised that should I feel the need to assist with the water bill when it came through – then that would be fine as well.

As I was moving out to go get a few grocery items for the home, I saw another female colleagues' response to my WhatsApp message. She in fact, thought I had a technical problem with my plumbing works so she recommended contacting a plumber so that he can come and fix the problem or share the concern with your landlord also to see what he can do for you. During our WhatsApp message exchanges, I asked her if she had her tap water working at home, she responded in the affirmative. This kind of brought good memories to me of a villa I had lived in for three (3) years, before I checked out of it. Whenever others do not have water, I have had my tap water running effectively. In fact, I became a water supplier whenever others have problems with tap waters.

Whenever you travel somewhere, enjoy the benefits on the ground

We had our sister-in-law who has come from Guinea and who was currently undergoing medical treatment. Good God, she likes every aspect of her presence in Dakar, except for one thing: 'Dakar is expensive for the average folk." However, she is only going to pay for her treatment, hence, she is going to shop her way around with the remaining money from her medical budget.

When money falls in the hands of willing spenders

Every one of us has needs to entertain. If we are not

careful, we will never have a dime savings in all our lives.

Watch! But don't criticize just like that

Sometimes observing something alone without proper inquiry will lead you astray, I was once opportune to observe two grown up men. One with the shovel and the other with the wheelbarrow, the one with the shovel was filling the positioned empty wheelbarrow and once it is filled, the other guy will empty the filed wheelbarrow just at the side.

These two gentlemen, from just observing without living it before or even experienced it before, you can quickly come to a conclusion that they are very stupid to waste their precious time just like that. I took my time to go through the chain of comments. Many of which was in fact a clarification that these guys are actually measuring the number of wheelbarrows required for them to do their mixture of a bag of cement and carry on with their job – the bricks making scheme.

In 2010, when I was constructing my house – I observed the same kind of stupid act as some of us may have seen it. To which, I patiently asked the laborers why are they wasting their precious time with this kind of a trend.

It is then, I was made to understand that it is not time they are actually wasting but rather following a scheme to help prevent too much of cement in the bricks or less of it in the bricks, but rather ensure that the bricks are of the proper standard for the purpose of the construction.

I argued with them, why they won't just measure how many shovels can they throw aside in order to get the proper mixture for the bricks? They respectfully answered me "Sir, it is not like that. Not all shovels are equal in size, the same with the wheelbarrows. So please let us just do our work the way we see fit? What you required of us, is to see your bricks in a proper state. Isn't that so?" I shamefully responded "Yes".

At the end of the day, I actually saw the sense in what appeared initially stupid to me after seeing the video clip on my Facebook timeline and the number of harsh comments leveled against these two guys. It got me concerned on how the whole world is quick to judge you for something, they have no idea of or no knowledge of, but just because they saw something they jumped to conclusions.

In over four decades or so in my life, I have gone through such reproaches – not exactly like the one   of the two guys on the construction site, but something similar. My simple warning to everyone; please always exercise patience to first learn and then get to appreciate the whole later on.

Sometimes we know a part and we think the person is qualified to take the credit. NO!

Early this morning, 11th July 2018, I realized the importance of an expression that I have never considered important but this day it meant a whole lot to me.

The rat race of the working class, one of my female colleagues walked in my office to greet me. All of a sudden we started discussing the ups and downs of work

> **Her**: *This is what we will be on until we go on retirement.*

> **Me**: *Yes, but you can go on retirement and think of being active as well. See the case of Mr. Freitas, who retired, but never got tired. He continued to be productive to date.*

> **Her**: *Yes, he is a man so he can do that not us women.*

Me: *No, Madam. It is not like that. What about Mrs. Candebo who went on retirement and later came to BACOCO and worked for close to 7 years again.*

Her: *Remember, she went on retirement at the age of 55.*

Me: *Yeah, but it is something for a woman of her age.*

This above mentioned response of mine got her tense and she provided this response for me.

Her: *Did she go through Maternity walls?*

Me: *To this one, I closed my mouth, because Mrs. Candebo did not go through that maternity wall throughout her life.*

So, she is not an example for any of us to bank on her exemplary tenacity concerning any working scheme.

The lesson I learnt from this discussion was this. Sometimes we know a part of something and then we draw our own flimsy conclusion from the little that we know. This also made me think about the Facebook video clip I saw, already alluded to earlier on where two gentlemen were making bricks so, please never be quick to judge or draw up conclusion when you only know part of the story.

Favorite Food or Good Food

There is a French adage that I learnt when I was a refugee in Gueckedou, Guinea, from one of my former colleagues, Mrs. Jeannette Yaradouno. She used to say: "Tout le monde, sait que sa bague, c'est en or." Meaning when translated: "A budget tells us what we cannot afford, but it doesn't keep us from buying it." - William Feather.

We all, one-way or the other, have things in our respective life that we don't hesitate to spend our hard earned money on. There are things that we will think first before we commit our financial resources on to buy them. Then there are things that do not require second thoughts for us to purchase them.

It is good to be in an environment and be very observant in order to be able to see the general mood of the people in that environment or community. This is how, over a long period of time I have interacted with the Nigerian community and I came to understand the meaning of two expressions ending with food.

1. Favorite food; &
2. Good food.

To any Nigerian I have so far known when the food is not to their local tastes, it is not considered as good food but if it is then it is good food. On 1st July 2018, on our way to Banjul, The Gambia, one of my Nigerian senior colleagues asked me if I do like Nigerian foods. To which, I answered Yes". One thing, he didn't also know about me, once I leave my home, I am open to any food in as much as the next person can eat and they are okay. Of course I can as well eat it and be fine. It is my philosophy and my own way of life.

Nigerians, by nature, regardless their station in life when it comes to their local taste of food – the food is classified in part according to the different states in Nigeria. This is something I also do in my own home but not in public places. The reason being, even if you washed your hands after having eaten that food the odor of the dish will remain, that for is a no go way area. I rather eat any food with cutlery and this to some Nigerians who have not experienced it before, will be considered as an insult to their culture.

Don't spend your time invest it is one of these commandments

On the 2nd of July 2018, I stepped out to take a walk while I waited for breakfast at 7:00am. As I walk through the Senegambia area, I spotted two guys.

1. A nuisance fellow – who told me he is a security officer; &
2. An airtime (recharge card) vendor, whom I respected a lot.

All of the sudden the one who told me that he is a security officer in the area approached me and asked what I was doing there? I told him that I needed a recharge card for Q Cell. Then came in the airtime vendor who was not only selling the airtime to me via a transfer service but guided me in how to go through activating many services on my Phone.

As soon as I left the spot to continue my walk the supposed security officer, followed me and requested me to help him get some money for his breakfast. Well, he has seen me pull out my wallet and pay out 250 GMD for just credit. In the process he also saw other notes as well, hence his request for help and I could not just go and leave without helping him out.

Just a few meters away from the spot where I had just bought the airtime. I heard a loud bang sound of a car accident. As I watched the scene because I had a few minutes still before breakfast time. Anyway after a while I started moving toward my hotel, the Senegambia Beach Hotel. As I am leaving, and to my surprise, the accident spot started attracting many idlers from all corners. . Even the recharge card seller left his business to go see what has happened, which was in fact the origin to writing this piece so that it can become a warning sign for people to be careful on how to use your time. You may be wasting your time unknown to you and sometimes you want to sympathize with someone or a passerby, and the like. Please be careful on how to go about this kind of sympathy.

Sunday Morning 1st July 2018:
Our mission to Banjul, Gambia

One of our office transport officials came to pick me up.

According to previous arrangements, we were supposed to pass by one of our colleagues to pick up the DSA (daily sustainable allowance) for the head of the delegation going to Banjul.

While on the way to pick up the Head of the delegation, I learnt two key lessons from the transport officer. I reminded him that our next colleague that we are supposed to pick is the one in charge of the conference and any interpretation that may be required. He handed me the completed forms, indicating though that his own form was not included

I then suggested to him that he call the one in charge of the transport unit as they started talking on the telephone I could follow the discussion, apparently it was discovered that the one in charge of conference had chosen to go to the airport at his own expense. He does not want to join the group due to the stipulated pick up timing.
Once at the Pied of the Monument de Renaissance Africaine; this officer chose to pass through the compound of the above-mentioned Monument. I thought it was not allowed but he said to the security officers at this monument: "This vehicle is a diplomatic vehicle, as we want to go the other way; could you please allow us to go through here."

The lady security officer opened the gate and we went through. This brave scene made me to immediately remember the book The Like Switch - Jack Schafer Ph.D, & Marvin Karlins Ph.D — January 13, 2015 that I have read some time ago and I have graciously been making use of it with my paperless (no particulars) vehicle I bought since October 2016.

When we reached the home of the head of the delegation, the said transport officer parked and said we wait till 11:00 am before I can notify him that we were around and waiting for him. I asked whether it would not just be okay for us to just let him know that we are here earlier.

He said no, we rather wait for the scheduled time to collect the Head of delegation. His point was that as we are working to take care of our families, we also want peace in our working relationship as well. So, let's wait.

I picked up my book Entrepreneur Revolution by Daniel Priestley to read. Just a few minutes later, the time was up. Then the head of the delegation called to find out if we were on our way yet, the driver confirmed that we were actually there already waiting outside.

Don't envy them, but rather pray for them.

I have always told my colleagues in my office there are a certain number of colleagues whose official working time is passed mostly via traveling. We all know to travel is enjoyable but as soon as it becomes a duty to earn your living then it is no longer comfortable. It is like having a very beautiful lady as wife and you are entertained by whenever you need her service. However, whenever the need has turned into an obligation that you ought to do otherwise you will not be in peace. Then it becomes a challenge and no longer a comfort.

Our head of delegation was returning from a mission in Paris around 1:00 am and was on his way again around 11:30 for another mission to Banjul, The Gambia – so it was back to back missions

To some of us who have not had a chance to experience such we considered it comfort but when he told the transport officer to stop by any available Pharmacy in order for him to get some medication. So that at least, he can be fit to make the journey to Banjul in good health.

There is no air up there

I was once opportune to watch, listen or read one of Guy Kawasaki's presentations. In his presentation, he said, those in top positions no longer have the energy to think properly due to their responsibilities and other duties in what they do. There is no time for them to invent anything. Information is no longer at their disposal. And even if they happened to stumble on some important information, due to their lack of time, it will be ignored.

The best way for them to operate well if at all they are willing of course, is to rely on those down below the corporate ladder to supply them with the right information, which will be a catalyst to stimulate their own mindsets.

This is a serious note to consider. Once you have moved up the ladder, note that several things will no longer be at your disposal like before when you were a hustler. You will need trustworthy folks to tell you or provide you with the right and useful information.

Are you also willing to listen?

Never underestimate the power of stupid people in a large group – George Carlin

I never knew this; every environment has this kind of group of people, let me say it again, we all ought to be very careful with them. My then office had this kind of group we used to call them – the group, it was a set of males & females and they were very purposeful in what they do. Little did some of us know their power, until I spotted the above-mentioned adage – then, it became clear to me to never again underestimate them.

"One man's choice is another man's neglect"

This is a Facebook comment I made on Bro. Kasory Samuwah's timeline.
  Please take a look on this, May God bless you? Amen. Remember, every nation has its own reality(ies). I was one day shocked by a Kenyan friend, all I knew before concerning my nation, Sierra Leone was her abject poverty, nothing else really.

Little did I know how beautiful Sierra Leone's beaches and her soil or environment that was the talk of the whole world, particularly for tourists who have visited Sierra Leone's beaches.

Here is a conversation between my Kenyan friend and myself whom I'll call for the purpose of this discussion KF & ME.

ME: *hey brother! How are you? I'm Comrade Fayiah LEBA.*

KF: *Oh bro. Comrade. I'm fine and you?*

ME: *Fine also.*

KF: *By the way, where are you from?*

ME: *I'm from Sierra Leone.*

KF: *Sierra Leone! The country that has capital called: Freetown?*

ME: *Yes, please.*

KF: *Oh Comrade! You have a beautiful city! Beautiful beaches, Oh how I wish I were a Sierra Leonean.*

You know the rest of the story of how he made me feel fine that day in November 2004

Since that day, I have changed my mindset and laid down my persistence criticism about how poor we are and started praying for the nation, her leadership and the populace. President Bio declaring his assets is a very good move. However have the former presidents of Liberia also doing the same thing please?

The nation of Liberia has come a long way to be where she is today. This was if my memory can serve me right, the nation that you could never point at her former President(s). Today, we can still see former presidents of Liberia. I consider that a good move on the right direction.

Instead of constantly pointing accusing fingers at the incumbent government (Gemawah's Administration) for their faux pas, start praying for it, you never know what that can do for the fragile nation like Liberia.

I continue to share with them by advising them to read his Bible well, please. I asked this question: Do you know the story of the persistent widow, please? Did she challenge the authority? Not at all, but rather continue to plead for justice in a loving manner. If you failed to do that, I'll do so. I will always pray for Liberia and her leadership regardless of what they are doing.

So continue in your negative mindset concerning things that are not working.

Remember the coin has three faces.

1. The head;
2. The tail; and then
3. The edge.

Stand at the edge of every situation in order to be able to see both sides.

Neglected blessings

Sometimes we are so blessed to a point because we in it always and due to familiarity, we do not see the blessings clearly until an outsider or a neutral person comes and let us discover God's blessing in our lives.

On 6th July 2018, one of my sisters-in-law (Mrs. NATO Angelic) came to Dakar for medical treatment, once in the lounge she discovered something she always pays dearly to have – the Internet.

This kind of discovery of the importance of the internet was first made by one of our sons, Tresor. He once told his elder brother, Ebenezer to stop downloading apps on the Android tablet they were using because this would deplete the data and they would lose the Internet connection. Few months later, he has gotten used to it

now and no longer sees it as important as before (in his early days in Dakar, where every horse he used to see would cost him to comment or exclaim.
The question by my sister in law that brought laughter to us is:

Is it possible for me to have this Internet Connection for 24 hours?

With laughter, my wife, Rose told her, "Yes, sister". She further went on to tell her that: 'Don't worry you will soon get tired with the constant internet connection." Many people around the world are making exploits on the internet today but I wonder whether you are making such exploits for yourself too?

Chapter Four

Faith!

Can it stand the test of time?

My family and I went to La Mie Fine Restaurant, because my wife said: "I am not in the mood to prepare dinner, hence, I will prefer for us to go get some finger food for our dinner this evening." Before we got there, we passed by the barber shop to have everyone hair done. Then later we went to the above mentioned restaurant but before we could get to this place, my two sons, Ebenezer and Tresor started their usual behavior of cat and dog relationship. Which if they are with me alone, I would not bother myself but I have a wife, who gives attention to details. When she does so, she wants to drag me in that hectic mode as well. Especially, she will spill out a foul language that I cannot hold on just like that but will be compelled to speak out.

Always, before I speak, whenever she spills out such foul language, I will tell her to mind her words. In fact, chiefly, I say to her – 'Mind your thoughts, because thoughts are things. Whatsoever we become gets its origin from what we spend most of our respective precious time thinking about."

While we were waiting to get our parcel to get ready for us to take home, it happened that the local TV of Senegal, La RST was on, and the topic of the day, was the World Cup. Which was been played in Russia 2018. The panelists' discussion was around Egypt been beaten by Uruguay: 0 – 1; Morocco also was beaten by Iran, the same score: 0 – 1. Then, the next match was between Spain and Portugal. Success leaves clues. Every one of the commentators on the panel discussion knew that the two countries were strong nations in terms of football. They have been World Cup holders. One statement got my attention that evening before leaving. One of the commentators thought that the game will end in a draw, I'm not actually a football fan but I wanted to see the success clue from what I heard from this man on TV that evening, how true those words would be?

As soon as I got home while my family was eating their dinner I quickly downloaded an App on my iPhone in order for me to get the scores of every match of the ongoing World Cup 2018. Exactly as the man predicted it, this is how the match went, it ended in a draw between the two soccer giants Spain & Portugal

This is the comment concerning Cristiano Ronaldo that pushed me to pen down this story: Portugal 3 – 3 Spain: Magical Ronaldo outshines mighty Spain with amazing hat trick
"Cristiano Ronaldo's stunning hat-trick earned Portugal a dramatic 3 –3 draw in their Group B opener against Iberian neighbors Spain."

What caused me to get attached to the statement of a stranger on TV was his accurate prediction of the match. He said because he has seen not once, not twice, not even thrice but several times the games of the two special nations Spain & Portugal. So, after having followed them for a while, it was now easy for him to come up with such conclusion, because success leaves clues for people to easily learn about the outcome of your game. When they see you play but you ought to provide for them some statistics that they can work around for their predictions.

People may be watching your output, so be committed and consistent in what you do. It is not easy to copy success. It will require a strong discipline. Are you that disciplined for you make a record like what Cristiano Ronaldo of Portugal has given the world to predict his success and it comes to pass?

Iron sharpens Iron

As iron sharpens iron, so one person sharpens another. Proverbs 27:17 | NIV

I have always learnt that for anyone to make a breakthrough in any life challenge, you ought to emulate those who have been there and done that.

Easy right? Wrong, it takes more than just emulating the successful people for anyone to be successful in life or be able to become that successful person you have seen and admired and want to be like.

We were travelling to somewhere, one of the tourist destinations in Senegal. As we were approaching our final destination, the enterprise discussion popped up. One of the participants said, he was surprised to discover that a barren land yesterday can today produce sweet mangoes through a simple watering of the mango trees. After that he engaged in a discussion around him being an entrepreneur. This saying got me interested, which pushed me to respond with the following question "Are you an entrepreneur or a wantopreneur [a wanna be entrepreneur]?

I went on to explain the meaning of the above-mentioned words. Entrepreneur is the person doing the act and is fully committed whilst the "wantrepreneur" is somebody wishing to become an entrepreneur, but does not know how to go about it. Many of us are "wantrepreneur" instead of entrepreneurs.

In most occasions and or events that we are invited to participate there tends to be surprises and lessons for us to learn from. Sometimes, it is through these kinds of occasions, we can meet our life partners. However, now the test of time comes, when the two of you have become life partners for real. Let me share with you a story that deserves sharing:

'During a vacation, a young couple signed up for a leisurely rafting tour down Georgia's Chattahoochee River. Dressed in sandals, a sundress, and a wide brimmed hat, they groaned when they discovered-contrary to the advertisement-that the trip included light rapids. Thankfully, they rode with another couple that had experience in whitewater rafting. They taught the husband the basics of paddling and promised to navigate them safely to their destination. Grateful for the life jacket, the wife screamed and gripped the plastic handle on the raft until they reached the muddy bank downriver. She stepped onto the shore and dumped water from her purse as her husband helped her wring out the hem of her soaked dress. They enjoyed a good laugh, even though the trip had not turned out as advertised.

Unlike the tour brochure, which clearly left out a key detail about the trip, Jesus explicitly warned His disciples that rough waters were ahead. He told them that they'd be persecuted and martyred and that He would die and be resurrected. He also guaranteed His trustworthiness, affirming that He would guide them toward undeniable triumph and everlasting hope (John 16:16-33).

Although it would be nice if life was easier when we follow Jesus, He made it clear to His disciples that they would have troubles. But He promised to be with us. Trials won't define, limit, or destroy God's plan for us, because Jesus's resurrection has already propelled us to eternal victory.

Lord, thank You for the promises in Your Word that assures us you've planned our path and remain with us and for us, no matter what comes.

There is this tendency whenever we see someone who has succeeded in what they know best. We want to be like them. Hell no! We have no idea how many hours of commitment and consistency this thing that the person does sometimes, effortlessly, took him or her to be where they are currently.

It will require strong commitment and consistency. Let's take a look on the story between Elijah and Elisha in the Bible. By then, for anyone to teach you a new trade in which you are not familiar with, it will require your whole life commitment and consistency before the person can also turn to you and teach you his or her tricks so that perpetuation is put in place. Today, the advent of technology has moved us from that, by buying our own way through a new lesson, which once learnt will catapult us to success, provided we are teachable or have a teachable spirit as well .

I have on several occasions refused to accept this theorem: "The 10,000-Hour Rule" which states that for anyone to be successful in any trade, you have to commit the above mentioned hours in terms of work, study, etc. before you can experience the longing success.

Can your faith really stand the test of time?

Browsing through the internet one day I read a strange but an amazing story of a clandestine church in Russia, which we all know anything clandestine in Russia, will hardly survive the test of time.

It was huge mixture of both supposed believers and the real ones. This went on for a while, then one day, a band of military officials stormed into the church building; the congregants knew it was not only the end of that church but their lives were in huge danger.

Scared for their lives, the church that was singing grew cold. The singing stopped and they were watching to see what was going to happen.

The commander leading the army shouted and said "

"All those who are for God and will prefer to die for their faith, should go on the right hand side.

And those who will prefer their lives and maybe someday they might likely worship or choose to be fervent in their dealing with godly things, should go on left hand side".

It was very few people who had the courage to go on the right to risk death because of their faith in God.

The majority choose the left hand side instead.

Then, the commander shouted that those on the left should bid their farewell messages to those who chose the right hand side because it will be the last time they are seeing them alive.

A moment of sadness flooded the auditorium and those who were on the left hand side did what they were ordered and they were later asked to go out and go to their respective homes.

Surprise sank in, as soon as those who chose the left hand side, left the auditorium, the situation changed in a positive manner.

The soldiers put their arms down and joined them to worship the true God with this statement: 'It's not good to worship God with hypocrites amongst you."

Now we know that all those who left were actually fake Christians.

Now let me ask you this simple but profound question: Can your faith stands the trial time?

It's easy to say I have a grounded faith when things are OK, but wait to prove it when the testing of time comes along that faith.

Faith in some cases is like this statement below:

"When you are going through something hard or a difficulty and wonder where GOD is, remember the teacher is always quiet during a test." If ever you have a faith that you are gaining something, let us say, tomorrow for instance, that is not a faith.

I can vividly remember a couple that was stripped off their benefit right, which was a telling blow to their wellbeing within a period of a year holdup. This move did destabilize their peaceful relationship, which made them drew closer to God.

Another story that drew my attention that early morning 13th June 2018 which I believe can also draw anyone's attention is a story of a toddler in Kindergarten class, the mom happens to be quick-tempered person while the dad was a slow to anger person. This toddler found himself amongst two different temperaments – one with hot tempered and the other, a calm type.

After the mom has dressed up the boy for school one morning, the mom observed that the boy was studying the Bible in search of two of Jesus' – a servant leader type and the one who is quick-tempered.

After having hurried up the boy into the car for them to leave the home for school, the young boy still had his question whether there are two Jesus. In the car, he now finally asked his question when now on their way to school.

"Mama, How many Jesus do we have in the Bible? She exclaimed, *"We only have one Jesus"* at which point he responded *'But my teacher told me there are two Jesus in the Bible".* This statement got the mom angry and she hurried up to school and went straight to the school administration to report this heresy observed in the life of her son.

The school administrator, the class teacher, the boy in question and his mom were in the Administrator's office.

"Who told the boy that there were two Jesus?" The Administrator asked. "It is my teacher" and the boy said, he went on to explain the reason there are two Jesus in the Bible. Jesus is our father, his children are supposed to behave the same like Him.

"My mom is Jesus's daughter but she does not do things like Jesus does because she lies, she fights with my dad. She pickpockets my dad, which is why I was in search of the Jesus that behaves like my mom in order for me to compare between the one my dad believes in and the other one my mom believes in. The one who behaves differently from what my dad does", the boy moved.

Before the boy could finish his explanation, her mom was already in tears covered with huge shame.

The reason I brought in this story is for us to be careful whom we believed in for the unanswered prayers. We may be a stumbling block to our own progress unknown to us. Do you have that faith, which is not reproachable? Many of us might be struggling due to our own behaviors. So let's be careful on how we behave.

Let your gentleness be evident to all. The Lord is near. Do not be anxious about anything, but in every situation,

by prayer and petition, with thanksgiving, present your requests to God.   And the peace of God, which transcends all understanding, will guard your hearts and your minds in Christ Jesus.
Philippians 4.5–7 | NIV

These are some of the ingredients that quicken our respective individual faiths. Never endeavor to be an enemy of progress to your faith in the God.

Faith! Oh Faith!

Where are you?

'But someone will say, "You have faith; I have deeds.
"Show me your faith without deeds, and I will show
you my faith by my deeds. – James 2:18 | NIV"

I don't know whether there is a relationship between hope and faith. However, there is no faith without deeds that will amount to anything good, so have the faith, all right, let your faith be accompanied with deeds, in order for Almighty God to bless the work of your hands.

Don't just expect something great and think that you can stumble upon it and there you are, you pick it up and make use of it like that. No. It does not work like that in any society. In fact, this is why African nations, many of them, got their Independence from their former colonial masters. Yet, many live in abject poverty. They failed to know that China was as well colonized. In fact, Hong Kong is actually part of China, but due to a bilateral agreement, she will only be handed to China and become a unified territory or part of the People's Republic of China, in 2047, God willing.

Today, this Asian nation is amongst the most respected nations on the planet. Why? The reason is that their faith was translated into serious action, which later got them to become a productive nation across the globe. They didn't depend on handouts and saw themselves as inferior.

There was a time, when I used to watch TV (from 2008 through 2013) then I gave up watching TV and switched to reading business books instead. I saw a mobile advert on TV, the kind of phone wherein you are able to watch a local TV station on and at that watch it free of charge! I also had a great craving to possess things, I mean, the latest things. When I was in Gueckedou, Guinea a senior colleague (Mr. Henry Korsor Sr.) who is now in Canada with his entire family used to call me with this salutation of Comrade, every new product in the market, I wanted to be in possession of that product. Today, the trend has changed.

So, I went in search of this smartphone, it is not like today when your Facebook account just by liking a local TV page, you will be allowed to watch things on the Internet for free. In one of the earlier stories, I made mention of the scene of the cassette and diskette, which have become obsolete today. The same will happen one day, when the TV will no longer be of value to the next generation, yet, many old school folks will hold on it and still cherish it.

First, I got into a Nokia phone shop, I asked if they had the above-mentioned phone for sale, the saleslady grudgingly told me "Sir! We don't sell Chinese products." This statement got me offended and in an angry mood, I answered: "Show me something in this room that is not made in China. Your wristwatch is made in China. Your polo tee-shirt is made in China. Even the jeans you have are made in China."

To everyone's great surprise, the strap of the jeans pant, it was written white-bolded characters: Made in China." Her colleagues could not hold back their laughter China turns their fragile faith into action, they own their own Google, Facebook, etc. People say, they are good at being copycats. Nobody invents anything, we all just need a platform, which we can turn things around and fine-tuned them and they become our own inventions.

How do I know that? I read it from a book Where Ideas Come From by Steven Johnson on the10[th] May 2010. This is where I learnt that ideas are just an early pregnancy and then become the child. Who grows to be a toddler and then gets to school age. All the way, to university and the child starts working for his or her money. If you are fortunate to fall on a graduate idea, you employ the graduate child idea into your company; they immediately start making money for you.

Some churches only depend on tithes and offering. I never knew that T.D. Jakes was an entrepreneur from birth before becoming a preacher. How do I know it? I read it from one of his Bestselling books SOAR! Great book, in fact it is through the same book, I learnt that in the US for instance amongst the black communities, the largest number of entrepreneurs are women. Don't be surprised by that, it is the soil (environment) that encourages that.

If any organization for it to thrive, it has to be a business based organization or, it has to have a business mindset. Lest it will have difficultly surviving the test of time, faith alone will not put food on the table for you, but let the faith be accompanied with little action in place, then the results will be excellent.

Some trust in chariots and some in horses, but we trust in the name of the Lord our God. Psalms 20:7 | NIV

Beware of who you trust or in what you put your trust. One afternoon during the month of Ramadan, when there was ten (10) days for the Muslim brotherhood to end their prayer and fasting period. Most colleagues will leave work to get home for other preparations. To be precise, the female colleagues for instance, were mostly fond of this early break of service to get home to their families' dinners prepared.

Between 14:00 to 15:00 GMT, the traffic jam on the roads was so high to a point I questioned the reason, why it is so? It is then, I was told that because of the remaining 10 days of the Ramadan prayer and fasting period.

The reason I am bringing this up, is this; whenever there is a Ramadan, 80% of restaurants in Islam dominated nations closed the service to the general public leaving no room for non-Muslims to eat their lunches. In fact, you are compelled to fast whether you like it or not. My many years in Senegal, have helped me adjust to the system of the land, now I do fast and pray in a Christian way instead.

In fact, the praying and fasting period has a threefold benefits for me as a person.

   ✓ Spiritually speaking, it draws me closer to the Almighty God and prevents me from doing anything funny that will not bring glory and honor to His Name;

✓ On the side of health, it helps to reduce some fat in my own body and bring some balance to my cholesterol. As we all know when you are healthy, it helps you save the health costs as well, which will now bring us to the third benefit – the financial aspect of it;

✓ On the side of finances. Whenever there is no fasting, on an average level, I spend between US$6 to US$10.00 daily from Monday through Friday on breakfasts, lunches or any other latte. This means, I spent nearly US$50.00 per week on food alone. If I have fasted for a week, the proceeds for that week can either go for good business books, or any charitable organization, such as church, and the like.

Life can sometimes be very difficult

I was once opportune to watch a small video on my Facebook timeline, wherein folks did carry a circular culvert to its final destination. Once there, they put two used motor wheels in order to offload the circular culvert from the truck that took it to its final destination. They had faith in what they were doing, however, to their dismay, as soon as the said object touched the two used wheels, it got broken into pieces. They stood speechless for a while and then assembled the broken pieces and moved on.

Sometimes, our faith or trust can put us into serious danger, which can cause us to either give up or never wish to try it for the second time or actually give up completely. In your faith, never lose hope as well. Sometimes, your faith or the trusted thing can fail you and if it does, summon courage and move on by giving it another try. Failure sometimes is a learning process. Remember this one message, all those who have made a breakthrough in their respective lives, it never occurred to them easily. Whenever you trust in something it is going to be successful, and if it fails you big time, never give up. For with failure we learn, while with success there is no lesson learnt, it is just quick celebration and then the process of working get started afresh.

Do you know FAITH intertwines with PATIENCE?

What a telling blow! Sometimes even dogs are more aware of dangers than some human beings. I was shocked with what my eyes saw on Thursday 7th June

2018. This is not a story I was told or someone explained it to me. No, I saw a video clip posted by one of Facebook family friend, bro. Adam Tongi, two creatures wanted to cross the busy traffic road and both the Caucasian lady and the black dog arrived at the zebra crossing and the pedestrian traffic light was on RED. Hence, the dog sat down to wait for the right time to arrive with the faith it will surely turn GREEN. Then it can seize the opportunity to cross on the other hand, the Caucasian lady was busy trying to go through the busy traffic and she was moving front and back which she actually managed to make halfway through. However, she could not complete the second phase, with the busy traffic road would not allow her to do so.

Do you see this scene between the lady and the black dog?

The lady was in haste to cross the zebra crossing with a mindset that the motorists will pause to allow her to cross, which didn't happen whilst the dog patiently waited for the traffic light to turn green and then majestically, move on to cross the zebra crossing. I could not believe what my eyes were seeing.

The scene made me to remember the clever biblical adage shown to humanity in the book of Proverbs, which goes like this: *"Go to the ant, you sluggard; consider its ways and be wise! It has no commander, no overseer or ruler, yet it stores its provisions in summer and gathers its food at harvest."* – Proverbs 6:6

What a lesson for me, whenever I'm pushed henceforth to be impatient with minor obstacles of life. I will now have to wait for the right timing. In fact, whilst waiting I need to be alert like what the dog did. It was very alert and as soon as the light turned green, it moved and got through the other side.

Many of us lack the patience. We are always running ahead of time and yet we claim to have faith. Is that really faith or impatient lifestyle? Next time, you are faced with little obstacles wear your faith and remember the story of the patient dog. Also, there is another clever saying: 'Patient dog eats the fattest bone 'Dogs are by nature, patient creatures – an attitude that has been established as an acceptable fact. It cuts across the board.

I never knew that for faith to have its full work there has to be a patient mindset as well, which can serve as a pipeline minister or a catalyst to achieving a great success in all that we do.

Chapter | Five

Why will you support someone?

In a world where everything we do today is commonly based on recommendations. Can anyone survive it without support or a slight push from someone? I hope we all know the adage: "No man is an island and no one stands alone." If I should expand on this above-mentioned adage; you can hardly make it in life without the help of others.

This can be your maid, your security, or even someone leaving their throne to you because it has been decreed by God. For instance the case of Jonathan and king David in our most clever and mysterious book, the Bible.

It was destined for Jonathan to fill in the throne position after his father Saul signed out but unfortunately for his dad who saw what his son was foregoing it to a supposed commoner, David, Jesse's son. I can say God used Jonathan as a David's Giant on whose shoulders he will gain access to the throne because Jonathan accepted to be used as the instrument to carry out this plan.

Where is your plan? If you have not found out your plan, it's in your mind. Tap into your precious mind and unfold your precious information that can turn you from an average individual to a VIP.

This is how I have unknowingly discovered constant progress in my life. One morning and to be precise, 21st November 2016; I woke up from my slumber with painful stomach cramp and I seized the marble toilet sit to remove the old one from down there. I sat and exhausted everything and gained some relief. I sat on my bed for the next evening sleep.

Because my normal time of waking up was 4.45 am GMT but from minutes after 3:00 am I was already awake so I went to the kitchen to prepare my solution: honey, lemon and dried ginger for the stomach cramps and as an energy booster for the day.

I was listening to the audio version of the book of Ezekiel in the N.I.V Bible. I finished and I tried without success to make a WhatsApp call for my daily devotion with my wife to be, Rose.

I sent a WhatsApp to her and had no response; I then called and she turned it off reminding me she is up and getting herself ready for us to start our daily devotion. While I was sipping my solution, all of a sudden, my audio book stopped notifying me that there is an incoming call.

Bang! She is the one calling for us to start our devotion and the topic of that day: What about you? Text: Ephesians 4:25 – 32.

After the reading of both the biblical message texts of the day, we sang the song:

Blessed be the name of the Lord

Blessed be the name of the Lord

Blessed! Hallelujah! Blessed! Hallelujah.

Blessed be the name of the Lord

After which, we prayed and later shared our daily messages and moved on. I returned to the kitchen to tidy up the kitchen.

I then, changed the listening of the Bible to a business related audio book listening. I tuned on the audio book

"Will It Fly? How to Test Your Next Business Idea So You Don't Waste Your Time and Money by Pat Flynn Narrated by Pat Flynn
6 hrs. and 27 mins
Unabridged Audiobook"

I dashed into the bathroom to take my bath naked as usual I grabbed my toothbrush and then toothpaste and as soon as put the paste on the toothbrush, the title: "Whose Glory, are you depending on?" of writing this eBook emerged and I went back to my smartphone and opened the note app to write down this above title.

Looking at things, I observed that I have more time to go, hence I said to myself; let me start writing my single page. Now before it is time for me to get ready to go to work

Naked I was, sat on the marble toilet seat and started writing, while I listened to the audio book mentioned above. I ceased the writing at 6:13am GMT because I was running out of time

After having taken my bath and dressed up and I still realized that I have at least 20 Minutes to start going to the office for that day work I again grabbed the smartphone and started writing. OK It's not a pen and paper writing, then let me say, typing with my fingers.

By professional standards, I'm a bilingual secretary which means I can type at least 60 words per minute but using a computer to type a note or a letter you are not in an office position is again becoming an old school stuff for many of us today.

Yet, many are still holding on to traditions. I've always told those I encounter in life's journey, be it in the street, in a queue at the bank, clinic, etc. If I greet you and you answered me; I will engage you in small talk in order for me to learn from that person. Also for that person too, can learn from me - it is a mutually beneficial type of thing. This is how I penned the title of another audio book in a lift going down in Beijing, China in April 2016.

While I was in the lift I met with a Caucasian, I knew I needed not to say 'Nihao!' but "good morning". Well she answered me and she was holding a physical book on her chest entitled: "The Leader in You".

To start a conversation with her, I said to her: "You must be a great leader from the look of things."

She cringed away and was not comfortable with such a cross joke but knowing how to fix things with anyone, I moved on saying: 'Don't mind me, it is the special book I saw with you that pushed me to say those things. Forgive me, I don't mean to offend you, please".

She said, "It's OK; I'm fine with that". But me wanting to continue the conversation, I continued and asked her: "Will you please allow me to take the title of this book?"

As it is spelt out in the clever book the Bible particularly in Matthew 7:7; once you asked, surely you will receive what you've asked for. So, please be wise in your quest, lest you receive something you are not willing to receive.

Before she even turned the book properly for me to copy the title, I've already taken the photo of the title. This is another lesson I learned from my son, Ebenezer when he was between two and three years. This young man taught me how to take pictures with your locked iPhone without opening it. Every time this boy grabbed my phone, in no time he will have filled my 32 gigabyte iPhone 4 with plenty photos. It is something I needed to learn from him but he was not willing to teach me because every time he grabbed my iPhone I would chase him take it away. From the past hard experience he once taught me whilst he was on my lap and he was sucking the poppy candy and he wanted to play with the computer whilst I was typing.

However, every time, he makes the move. I will stop him and the scene went on for a while and he was not comfortable with it. He got angry and bang! He hit the screen of the Toshiba notebook computer and everything went blank and I could not see the text I was typing. The screen got spoiled and now I have to fix it as he now says, it's not funny.

To get this screen repaired, I was charged a sum of 150,000 francs CFA. In the process, I was obliged to learn the hard lesson of coping with a toddler in our current BAC (born after the computer) world of our nowadays children. Some of us are the BBC (born before the computer) offspring. This is how I learned from an online course on managing your busy and working life with your toddler. It's there I came to understand that when you're dealing with a toddler. They don't like the phrase: 'Don't touch." If you were use it, then you have given them the excuse to find a way to now touch and because of the awareness of "don't touch scene", they will either damage what you have forbidden them to touch or the thing you have forbidden to touch will damage them – either way one thing will happen.

Hence, you allow them to touch it and even play with it, but you monitor the process. This is how I was able to teach him how to turn the gas off and on, when his mum was all the time chasing him out of the kitchen.

On Monday, 21st November 2016, Ebenezer tentatively moved to our home through the help of family friends from Sierra Leone.

You see sometimes, time is the perfect healer in any situation. My ex-wife, when I was moving and leaving her I called her and told her I am leaving you and will want to move to my new home with Eben, our son.

She had this question to me: "When your mom was leaving your dad, did she leave you with your dad?"

I answered her, negative. "So, then, my son is not going to live with you because my children are the only ones to comfort me in this divorce situation." She said.

Me, by nature; I'm a peace abiding folk, I let go the request, but I know time will tell us who is capable of handling this young man.

In the Judge's both temporary and final decisions, he ruled that the boy remains with his mom, according to laws. As we all know, wherever, two people of different sexes are in battle, favoritism is always or most often played in favor of the female counterpart. Because, even the Bible also considered them as weaker vessels, hence favor is always at their doorpost.

However, there is a thin line between logic and reality. *'In fact, not everything that is true is a reality, but a reality remains to be true."* What are the norms and the reality at stake are two things diagonally different in perspective. This is the mistake every one of us makes and then, we regret later on in life.

Sometimes, you see a great organization and you tend to wonder what is keeping this organization intact or still an exemplary type.
Some may think it is its leadership.
Some may think it is its infrastructure.
Some may think it is its system.
And still some may think, it is its people.

With this, I mean, the people. I will partly agree. Sometimes, Human Resources can make your organization stand out as an exemplary type, or break it and make its image. Depending on the type of people

you have and how their behavior has been incorporated
into the following:
- ✓ The leadership;
- ✓ The infrastructure;
- ✓ The system; and
- ✓ The people (the key to break or make).

This morning, 27th November 2016, Eben and I clashed
on the drinking of water early in the morning as soon
as he wakes up.

This is how I'm currently trying to fix certain things in
the life of the young lad, Eben. This same morning,
when he woke up and I offered him half-glass of water
to drink

Eben: "I'm not thirsty"

Me: Yes, I know, but you need to drink it.

Eben: For what, he angrily asked?

Me: Well, you see Eben this is what Papa takes
daily and he's always healthy and there is no
doctor's visit. I shared with him.

Eben: OK

He drank the water and moved to sit down and I then, offered an apple to eat without even brushing his teeth.

Eben: What! Are you kidding me, right? He questioned.

Me: No, my dear it's medicinal. Just give it a try and you will see the results soonest.

Eben: Can someone come and get me out of here, he exclaimed!

Me: You want to eat bread and egg, right?

Eben: Yes, please.

Me: Then, you have to eat this apple first or else, even if I prepared it you will not eat it.

Him, knowing me, of doing what I say, he just gave in (surrendered) and ate the one apple, while I prepared for him and myself some breakfast.

This is a message from the book of Proverbs Chapter 22 verse 6 "Start children off on the way they should *go, and even when they are old they will not turn from it.*

I've started implementing it in his life.

Sometimes, it is very difficult to continue things if you are not a disciplined person. I started writing this Book, but later stopped not because of lack of ideas, but many things cropped up serving as a stumbling block

The TRESOR's Way of life

Hey! My bonus son Tresor, a son not like others as for smartness, he's very smart. The first day, I saw this young man in July 26, 2015 in Conakry, I cherished him immediately and the mom by then, who was my business partner; shared her challenges with me in the upbringing of this young man.

Tresor was very smart, but he lacked cooperation. He's very jealous, hence, in everything, he only wants it for himself and his mom interpreted this as a sign that this child will make it in life. To which, I responded that it is a failure we ought to correct as parents. Because it will be very wrong for him to have such a mindset and think of succeeding in life.

It was on Monday, 12th December 2016 with Groupe Trans Air from Conakry after our wedding of the year. He was so happy to see himself off the soil of Conakry, however, once in Dakar and meeting with Ebenezer, for him, the dream of loving Eben, immediately became a nightmare for him, because he wanted his way, and he found himself with too many don't rules:

- ✓ You don't stick out your tongue;
- ✓ In this house, there aren't two moms nor two dads, hence, calling Mama Rose or Papa Comrade are no more, please. OK, please?
- ✓ No petty complaints;
- ✓ Etc.

But as with every child you put your rules and fail to follow up on them. They will be written rules placed in either a placard or cupboard but if care is not taken, they will never be implemented. On the contrary I am, by my nature what most people call a 'Follow—Talk" Graciously, I have thus far, done what I say I will do and for this, I am very grateful to the Almighty God for such stance in my personal life.

This is the fine night, after we have gone through the daily toiling. My wife, Rose has done the cleaning of our two bedroom apartment the cooking and the like, she was so tired. That night she humbly requested that she be exempted from any love making. Me, being an understanding husband, I agreed to her plea.

Unfortunately for both us, we immediately felt asleep and forgot to monitor the waking up of our two young gentlemen:

- ✓ Ebenezer
- ✓ Tresor

Between 2:00 and 3:00am, I remembered to wake up and go get them to pee. To my disappointment, I see that Eben has already peed in the bed. Yet I asked him to wake up to pee. I asked him to take off his clothes. I also, asked Tresor to wake up and pee, he also did as requested. Usually, it was first come — first served but this time it was first come — last served. It was Eben that woke up first, but last served because he had to be cleaned up. Hence, I requested Tresor to go back to bed on his dry spot and allow me clean up Eben.

After Eben, has cleaned himself up and was now ready to get back to sleep. Obviously he needed a clean place to sleep. Unfortunately for him, he needed to now lay his body on a wet spot. I thought of taking up his towel and lay it on the wet spot in order for him to manage it like that till the next early morning for us to find a way out.

As I was arranging the towel on the wet spot Tresor being the complainer as usual raised an alarm: "Stop disturbing me Eben." Unfortunately, Eben is still cleaning up himself in the toilet and wearing his clothes. So I told him that it was me, and I asked him to push to his place in bed and stop these petty complaints of his. He was shocked, because he thought it was Eben that was arranging the wet spot.

According to the French slogan: "Bête noir" which when translated means 'Looking for unnecessary problems', he seems to be the only one to be in control.

In the below mentioned response to his uncle, wherein his uncle's congratulatory message to us for our gigantic wedding in Conakry, he did a gentle tease, which turns out to be a great concern altogether: 'Please greet my jealous nephew."

This is a situation that I did share with his mom, but she saw it as a mark of success to which I dismissed and shared with her that we ought to do something about it because it will become something very serious for him tomorrow, if it is not handled now.

The special response to Tresor's uncle (Sahr Mando Tamboukende)

"Jacques!

A good one there. I never knew that you had such wisdom for an unmarried folk to know how to counsel a couple.

This is the world we are currently in. With the advent of technology, our grandparents who were born before the computer (alias: BBC) and didn't endeavor to learn the current technologies, the current state of life has rendered them obsolete.

And those, born after the computer (commonly called BAC), and when they are equipped technology-wise. They are wiser.

I can now understand the angle you are coming from. You're the BAC (born after the computer) and are well equipped. Hence, you are now qualified to counsel us as well.

Thank you. Your jealous nephew is faring well, relatively. He's striving to adjust his life to the reality of the day.

Today, whilst we were driving home from church, he gently asked the mom, when will they be going back to Conakry.

His mom said, my son, relax — this is our new home. Get used to it, please.

He went further, when Cathy and Fatou would come here? Not to my knowledge, his mom said. For here, he does not have the freedom to visit any neighboring children without permission.

Hence, he's seeing that little discipline as a serious issue to cope with, you know.

Our prayer, is for us to become an exemplary couple; not for evil deals, of course, but good deals, to the glory of God, Almighty

Folks! There is something in the name you give your child. There is something in whose name your child is named after. It's got me concerned when I saw Jacques full name in his CV.

I raised the concern with the elder sister, Rose who was by then, my business partner only and the outgoing Managing Director of ETOFAWAR Guinea.

I had wanted to change Jacques' full name, which is still like this: Sahr Mando Tamboukende, to be modified. She grudgingly moved, you tell him. I shared my concern also with Jacques himself, not only he was adamant with my suggestions for him to dropping the Tamboukende.

I didn't stop there I moved on to also share the same concern with his own dad.

Two key things, he did share with me that were important to him. "The Tamboukende name is my father's name and in remembrance of him in my life, I chose that name for my son, Jacques." His dad moved.

Also, changing it now will incur costs, finally conceded to this request

The cost! I was ready to take up the cost, but as the clever saying goes: 'Never dance where you are not allowed to dance."

So, I backed off with the concern of changing Jacques' name by dropping the Tamboukende name in his full name.

Let me share with you the meaning of Tamboukende name. It's a nick name or a common expression with close friends, which you are known by the community each and every one of us find ourselves in.

Like in my office, most colleagues call me: Commie, when my real name or full name is: Comrade Fayiah LEBA.

However, the name Tamboukende is a Kissi expression, which means a person of bad character and this bad character is so strong in the person's life that they will never change from that bad character.

You see why I had wanted the issue of bad character to change in Jacques' life?

We could have passed through the legal procedures to dropping the Tamboukende name. However, I met the obstacle of no go area.

Today, parents, and elder sisters are currently complaining that Jacques is so selfish. Well, it's in his name. For it is not Jacques' fault. Bad character of either selfishness or any other bad character is seen in his name. The best of Jacques is yet to come for they have not seen anything yet.

According to the dictionary definition for the word: JEALOUS – showing extreme cupidity; painfully desirous of another's advantages (covetous, envious).

We are currently striving to change the thought of Tresor.

'Be careful of your thoughts, for your thoughts become your words. Be careful of your words, for your words become your actions. Be careful of your actions, for your actions become your habits. Be careful of your habits, for your habits become your character. Be careful of your character, for your character becomes your destiny. – Chinese proverb

I call it: TWAHCD (Twahcad or the thought – the fountain of life).

Chapter Six

Resist the devil

Easy temptations, the Delilah syndrome on your way to success

Be Inflamed To Conquer
In doing so, resist the devil to conquer.

A hunter will only shoot a bullet at a time, whilst for a machine gun the one shooting it can get out several bullets at a target. The target can be smashed in pieces in no time.

Most times it's not everything that happens to us which comes from the devil. This has made some of us give the devil a very important place that he does not deserve. Note this well. You and I are constantly in a spiritual battle with the devil. Many things that happened in our lives, though the devil had his hand in some of them, he is not always the one to blame.

When we see diseases constantly or there is a reoccurrence of bad situations in your life concerning a particular disease. Sometimes, it might be the food we are eating, which might be the cause to that health challenge.

Let me tell you what happened to me some time back, I discovered very late particularly in my early 40s that I had cholesterol, which was killing my sexual desire gradually also the stress of an unhealthy marriage was there. The office politics was as well killing me softly.

I thought of tackling my problems one at a time, I started a divorce process with my now ex in order for me to save the life of my son, who was so dear to me, and whose life I never wanted to lose just because of the bad marriage. So, I chose to sacrifice my shame and even finances in order to save his life for he was precious to me.

I then, gave up the staff representative position in my office, and concentrated my efforts in bringing healthy life to my newfound family. After having divorced and in six months remarried though with strings attached it was worth the sacrifice. I am very much grateful to God for that step, which others saw was a wrong one but it was the right direction for me.

There is a clever Nescafé slogan: "If you have not tasted it, you will never know if it is good." It is easy to point accusing fingers into others' faux pas, but relax. You wait and see yourself in such first before you can endeavor to figure out how it hurts.

After having divorced and remarried in less than a year's interval and refrained from any office politics. I then moved on to watch or observed my eating habits. One of my sons Eben used to tell me: 'Papa, you ought to do gym to reduce your belly. It's too big." In early 2017 I discovered what I needed to do but as we all know, bad habits died very hard. I was at the same time also going through several crises. My new wife, Rose was just going through several miscarriages. To a point she even accused me of not knowing how to make love with her in order to keep our lost pregnancies which is the cause of all the miscarriages she was going through, to which I told her not to speak like a woman that lacks common sense. Glory be to God today, that stage has become a history and we are currently waiting for a bouncing baby boy to be soon born in December 2018, God willing Isn't God wonderful?

The moods, you wake up and observe that you don't want to talk to anybody. Check yourself some of those moods are the devil's activities you must be carrying out on his behalf. It is not important for you that you are ignorant, but they are the devil's activities. In the word of God, if you are dealing with the devil, resist him. Refrain from participating in his activities.

Be vigilant, be sober minded. God's desire is for you to overcome the devil. If you're not ready to take the challenge, the devil will never relent to do so, every time there is an opportunity to do his job so, you ought to be very much alert.

Greater is He that is in us, than the one in the world. Resist him! Hear me well, the one who's sinning is from the devil and he is doing the devil's activity instead of doing God's job and be blessed. God's good work is to destroy the work of the devil, the Lord God sent His son, Jesus Christ to the world in human form.

Also, remember we are in spiritual warfare with the devil. John the Baptist was a great man of God, but via the command of the little girl, he was beheaded so, you see what the devil is capable of doing if you are not careful with life challenges? We then ought to resist him. Stand against or oppose what is evil in your midst. You may be seen as ugly today, but time will heal the process along the way.

Let us say for instance, an invasion is coming into your life, you either stand against it or oppose it, if not you are dragged into it and be humiliated.

To prevent you from such, let your actions and words be Christ-driven and seasoned with the word of God in a prayerful stance such as this phrase: Satan! By the word of the Most High God, I resist you in the name of Jesus.

In any event, if you have been slandered, let this kind of statement come out of you *"I'm not like that, but a child of God."* Be your piece of word and move on in life. Not everyone will love you anyway. If Joseph had his own brothers as enemies because of sharing his life dreams with the family; who are you not have enmity in your life as a human being. However, we are called to resist. Stand firm don't be weak

How do you resist?

Submit to what the Bible teaches about the devil. Many of us are living by what people say not what the word of God says. Let me share with you.

There was a time, some friends were travelling from Lomé to Accra in a vehicle and they got themselves into a discussion. Everybody was saying 'Mammy water''. As it happens, there was a little girl amongst those travelling on this trip. The little girl kept calling to her mother for water constantly. As the discussion went on (the little girl by then was 6 years old) asked one of the passenger in the vehicle, who happened to be her dad and said: 'Papa, if there is mammy water, what about pappy waters?" The question aired to the dad brought a dead silence to this group of believers in Christ Jesus. It was a moment of reflection. This story of mammy water was just an imagination found in this west side of Africa, which is a practice very common in our societies. Let's be careful with what we have been saying to ourselves or considered to be a true story, for instance this story of mammy water.

It is written:

Satan in a Hebrew language means adversary. Know that Satan is a fighter. Diabolos criminally charges you. He comes to destroy your character regardless of your status. When he was Lucifer, he was an angel. When he lost his place in heaven as one of God's angels, he became Satan. He was an angel, he was powerful, and he is still powerful but without Jesus we cannot resist the devil. I can stand in the blood of Jesus, to resist the devil.

You are the adversary to the devil. He is never there for you.

Whenever you want to doubt the word of God then, the process of carrying out the devil's activities is starting to work in your life. Whenever you say: "But", You are trekking in the devil's zone. He is deceiving you to doubt the word of God. Remember, the devil is the liar.

There are Christians, they even speak in tongue. However, whenever they open their mouths to speak check and make sure you have the following things to get what they are saying:

1. Wisdom;
2. Knowledge;
3. Understanding; &
4 Discernment.

But you can straight away discover that they are not saying the truth. They are Christians, of course, but a double standard type. Nothing good comes from their mouths.

Love the word of God with all your heart, soul and mind. Satan parades like an angel of light. In fact, the Bible says he was the most beautiful angel. So, never be fooled that the devil is ugly and seen as a monster. No, the devil looks very beautiful in most cases. It is for you to be fearful of it that the world has cartooned him to be a monster. It is not so in reality.

Humble yourself to the word of God. Be careful. The devil parades himself like an angel of light. Be careful, the devil works around right now as you are reading these words. It is because he resisted righteousness that he was banned in heaven to stay. Note that he reports to the Almighty God.

You must be willing to resist the devil in your life. Nobody can do that for you. It is a personal decision. Satan uses counterfeit signs and wonders. Can you relate to the story of Moses' first miracle of a staff turning into snake and the Egyptian magicians did the same by throwing their staffs as well to become snakes? Unfortunately for them, the snake of Moses swallowed up all the magicians' snakes. You see the difference for yourself now?

It's not every miracle that comes from God. Satan can tempt you to sin, however, when you're tempted, flee from the temptation, but resist the devil. Don't resist here, but run away. Don't say, I can spend a night near a beautiful lady naked near me who is not your wife, nothing can happen. There are ways, or things you need not to resist but run away from them.

'Have you noticed my servant, Job'? (Job 18) God recommended Job. Most often, today none of us wants to be recommended to Satan, by God due to Job's tough experience. Sometimes, we are oppressed. Don't see somebody going through hard time, and rebuke him of sinning or you will say, God is rewarding them for the evil they have done to people in life. No, never do that. First examine and if possible, pray for them, instead.

Maybe it's the process of developing the person into a new person like in the case of Job.   On a personal note, I will resist the devil and stand with Jesus. Let's take an instance wherein you have been quarreling with your spouse, this quarreling is never ending. Either both of you may be carrying out one of the devil's activities; unbeknown to both of you or one person has given the devil a foothold into their life firmly. Resist the devil. There are many things the word of God teaches already. Submit to the established authority of God. There is therefore no condemnation to those in Christ. Let's just submit ourselves to Him.

Nothing can separate us from the love of God. In all these things, we are more than conquerors. God sent

His Son, to save us. All that is required of us is to submit and to be vigilant about spiritual warfare. Watch over your life. It's not good for a Christian to give yourself to alcohol. You should not be filled with wine. Don't be anointed by alcohol. Be inflamed by the Holy Spirit, instead.

Some people when they have a problem, they drink and go to bed drunk. However, they fail to know that as soon as they wake up and once sobered the problem remains unsolved. Whereas, they could have reflected over the problem and see how best they could initiate the problem solving abilities and forge ahead step by step. Stop making excuses for yourself, whenever you have a bad day and lord it over your family members. Stand against it and discipline yourself and exercise self-control.

Chapter | Seven

Renewed Mindset
(Mentality)

Do not conform to the pattern of this world, but be transformed by the renewing of your mind. Then you will be able to test and approve what God's will is—his good, perfect, and pleasing will. - Romans 12:2 NIV

Brethren, you see, life has its own ups and downs. However, you ought to be alert and ready to learn and unlearn certain things. Knowledge alone is not that useful as you learn, think of putting all your little knowledge that you have learnt on a daily basis into practice. Some may have side effects and others will be excellent for you. I am not saying you will not have problems but for every issue at stake, you will already have an anchor to serve you as a pipeline minister or catalyst role to either walk you through or serve as an obstacle to reconsider your steps.

I was once opportune to watch a video entitled the 25% scenario that is been divided by 5. Obviously, for what the scripted scene has taught us in schools - *the answer after having divided 25 by 5, will be 5.* No doubt about it. However, if there is a lack of consensus, though the real answer will be 5, majority will not accept it. Remember, the danger the world has today is called: Democracy. In societies where things are considered norms, maybe it might work for them. However, anywhere there is no rule of law, it will be very difficult for democracy to be the element of consensus.

Sometimes, many of us - particularly in our minds, can have such conflicting scenes. Speak to yourself. Relax. This is why we are sent to school to learn how that system works in life and that system has kept many of us at the same position in life. It is called conformity we are all called to conform to the system at hand. Anyone who fails to do so is considered either a half-caste or an unscrupulous fellow.

Let me also tell you that sin, by nature is very sweet. If you are not careful, you will never ever consider certain things to be very bad. Either for your health or morally for that matter, once you have learnt that it is wrong for your health to smoke, maybe when you started smoking you just did it for pleasure. However later on, in life, you learnt that it was not good for your health. Extracting yourself from the smoking habit becomes a serious task to carry out. That smoking pattern becomes something you are going to fight for life, if you are not strong in your decision making.

Do you know how to transform a critical situation in your favor?

During the early morning rush hour, after dropping my son to his school there is something I came across. From my son's school to work there are roughly ten (10) crossroads and every one of these crossroads requires tactfulness and a patient minded person, lest you end up in an accident with either a pedestrian, a taxi-driver or another vehicle. On the 5th crossroad, I spotted a lady in her sky blue Honda car coming on my far left hand side. I knew, before she could overtake me, I would be well ahead of her. But she was very tactful. She waved and smiled at the taxi-driver on her left hand side and did the same to me. I felt this to be intriguing, so I observed further, as she, with smiling thank you notice, she slowly moved between us. It was so good that it made me to pull over in order for me to record the event and who knows where it might serve me in the nearest future. So jokingly I would refer to this scene in the future, at the braveness of one woman who employed a tactic to turn a situation to her advantage.

Mind renewals a process to be considered seriously, there are a whole lot of clichés in any individual's life that need a great strategy in order for them to be amended. The first thing one can spot that needs urgent attention or an immediate change can be a badge of old school friends. It might be difficult for many of us to leave old but very good friends for any other thing in life.

Hey! You want me to leave my childhood friends for such and such. Is it worth the effort for anyone to do just that? Yes, put yourself in their shoes and say: *"Let your gentleness be evident to all men, particularly in responding in terms of difficult situations".* Let it be with tactfulness; For instance, one can put it like this "not so, sir/madam" but rather refrain a bit from sharing with them every bit of the private discussions, instead. Giving out old things or letting go of old stuff is sometimes very hard, with no remorse, they would categorically say to you 'No I can't, I will not do that!'

 A question might be thrown out to them in order to know the reason, behind their non—negotiable stance. It will surprise you to hear that they will advise you are the right person for me, they grudgingly moved.

Most often, it is good to have frictions from the early stages of any relationship that will thrive in future. This will help both partners to learn to know the grey areas or no go areas in each and every step that needs to be taken if at all it is bound to succeed. In fact, in life, there are three kinds of people in relationship, particularly, in relationship that are bound to remain permanent and they are as follows:

- ✓ Those who can initiate it, but are not willing to burn the midnight oil with you;
- ✓ Those who can initiate it and mend it for a period of time and later give up, yet want to be recognized for their early commitment;
- ✓ *Those who not only initiate it, but water it for it to grow so that they can eat of the fruits, after which, they will prone it and with commitment and consistency, they will grow it from glory to glory and not a single day they will relent their efforts to see to it that everything is in a systematic order for the wellbeing of that relationship.*

Why the 3rd group of people succeed in their endeavors? Because they keep on working on their relationship and never walk out of the learning school so that their relationship can gain new grounds and improve for the better daily lives. It is called the **strategy of daily commitment and consistency.**

What do you do, when people do not want you to move forward in doing things, unknowing to them, but they systematically become a stumbling block for those around them?

One day, I watched a small YouTube video entitled: Name a stubborn driver, but the name of the blog is: Bad Drivers. It was a huge traffic where lanes were opening by turns for the deadlock traffic to flow. Few drivers, who were hooked in the deadlock traffic jam, chose to move on the open lane to move faster instead. In the process, a driver in a grey KIA vehicle, moved to the open and fast lane when their own lane was awaiting eventual opening to block any vehicle passing them while they were waiting for their own lane to be open.

It was not funny. He was not moving at all and the drivers of the cars carrying commuters lining up behind the stationary vehicle chose to come out their vehicles and talk to him/her. The person that took that quick recording was a bit far from the stationary vehicle so we could only hear the noise in the background. Actually, people lining up behind the stationary vehicle were getting off their vehicles to come and plea with the owner of this vehicle to move on so that others stalked behind will also move.

The scenario went on to point where the now stationary vehicles started moving because the one at the blocked lanes have gained the opening and traffic jammed vehicles started moving, yet, the same vehicle was stationed and was not moving.

Gradually, the people continue to come see the vehicle owner and plead, until the stationary vehicle owner judged it necessary to move on and then the traffic gained its normal flow of things. Imagine, if anyone that was in that traffic was now going for a job interview. Will the interviewers believe his or her apology for arriving late to the interview? I doubt it.

The scenario was not horrific parse but it was interesting to me because it actually relates well with what I have thus far lived before and the comment below the title there was another short line: *Do you know somebody like this?* This incidence took place in London. One single comment that grabbed my attention: *"We all know one!*

Who are you blocking in your life? How often do you stand before people's progress? The scenarios may be different from the above story but each of us knows someone who thinks you cannot progress. That should not bother you if it does bother you; you actually make a grave mistake. People can tend to block you for some times but they will finally end up giving up and let you move on. One quick lesson I personally learnt from the scene, though the vehicle owner had attitude problem, those who came and talked to him or her remained very cordial. They chose to be polite with him/her.

When things go wrong or when things don't go the way you wanted, are you that polite? It was no longer the waiting in the queue of an open lane traffic that matters but the polite attitude displayed by those the scene affected. Take this when Jesus Christ was crucified on the Cross of Cavalry. There were two robbers who were crucified with Him. One on His left, and then the other on His right hand side; one got his visa to heaven, while the other got his to hell. Two people, right? All robbers, one went to heaven while the other straight to hell fire. Why? Attitude, it is not what happened that matters, but your attitude toward the incidence that counts. Good attitude is a mindset, and bad one is also a mindset. On which, your mind is set? If your mind is set on the positive side of things, then, your mind is gradually renewing itself. Strive for that.

I was once favored to read one of T.D. Jakes' books. This is not a religious book. It is an entrepreneurial book. It is entitled: SOAR! As I combed through the book, I discovered that he is more an entrepreneur in pastoral clothing. The book, SOAR! Teach more of flying the plane in figurative terms than driving a vehicle around in major cities in the world. It is also through it I discovered that there are more African American female entrepreneurs in the USA than their male counterparts. When I discussed this with my best friend, she told me – it is normal because women are marginalized in the USA more than in any part of the world, though it is considered one of the world superpowers. A discussion that triggers into another scene, which pushed me to ask her: How do you know this? She answered me. I read it from your plenty books you stalked me to read in order to be business oriented person like you. That discussion made my day because she was chipping off her own old way of thinking and doing things and grasping new things and believe me or not, such friendship can last for a very long time because both parties are gradually gaining solid ground with the help of the Almighty God.

Quick anecdote: This friend in her old lifestyle, if you wanted her to do anything formidable, you have to be very tough with her. To which, I considered such stance as very brutal. In preference, I rather encouraged than forced people to do things, even if it is for their own good. To which, she always said: *The use of your soft power and not imposing your stance as the man of the house, has led you to fail in your previous marriage."*

The above statement, I can identify myself with it. It is my reality. Actually, I used to be very brutal in my dealings, but later found out especially since the day I gave my life to Christ or considered Him, as my Lord and personal Savior, in February 2001. It is then, and there I started moving from being brutal in my dealings to encouraging instead.

Unfortunately, I became someone I was not understood by my then family. If the Almighty God was not brutal with the people of Israel, and forgave them every time they turned to Him and asked for forgiveness. Who am I not to choose that path? If at all, I am created in the image of God.

Apart from tribes, nations, internal conflicts, etc. People engaged themselves with these conflicts, however, after having fought for a long time, they will still end up on the peace table to talk it over and find consensus. Why not begin there in the first place?

Do you know your rush hour?

For some of us that drop off and pick up of our kids from their respective schools know the periods of these rush hours.

However, whenever you discovered there is a fake traffic jammed in the afternoon, let's say, between 2:00pm and 3:00 pm local time. Know this. There is either an accident or a presidential motorcade, which is also a recipe of unnecessary traffic jams commonly called fake traffic.

Anything that is artistically and appropriately done regularly in-front of people will attract attention.

Particularly in-front of the younger generations nowadays this is how Simon, and Baptiste, my son, Ebenezer's classmates have introduced a special greetings every time we meet with them in their school.

Baptiste will give me an Igbo cultural greeting, whilst Simon will provide the greetings, but will demonstrate a special scene that required the attentions of his classmates.

Initially, it was ignored, today, it has become a scene they now expect to see every time I'm in school to either drop off or pick my son. Simon and his parents are supposed to leave Dakar to move to France, where he would continue his primary education and then, secondary one.

This kind of the above scenes in action if kept in practice in a committed consistent action are called: "systems."

Sometimes systems can ruin a life of an individual, if the system in itself is a poor one. It also can elevate, if it is a better one.

This is how my wife Rose is gradually getting rid off certain practices which she used to consider important in her yesterday years and they are gradually becoming obsolete, for the mind is gradually becoming renewed.

One of it was street dining. Oh how she did love that practice! When we were courting or I was dating her newly. In Conakry, whenever I'm around and we are moving around the city.

In fact, she was not used to taking breakfast in the house, because she depended on her street eating, which was more appetizing and very appealing to the eye like Eve's fruit of life and death sin in the Garden of Eden.

"Rome was not built in a day." An expression which derives its origins from the usual English translation of a

medieval French phrase, «*Rome ne fu[t] pas faite toute en un jour.*»

It can commonly be broken down into this adage as well: "Anything of value will require time and patience or it is not earned easily."

We all know mind renewal, whether good or bad hardly get renewed easily. So to get changed mindset, it will obviously require enough amounts of patience, committed counseling and consistent tactful follow-ups.

On this fine Friday, 23rd March 2018, my wife, Rose had a medical appointment at Clinique de la Madeleine with her gynecologist.

Once at the clinic, we went in search of a parking spot not near the clinic, but a distant away from the clinic.

After having parked properly, we checked out of the car and start walking to the clinic. All of the sudden, she spotted an eatery where good breakfast was sold.

Oh Baby! You know, I didn't take a solid breakfast like what you did at home. You usually take a king's breakfast and a rich one, which can take you throughout the morning hours, until the lunch time is up. She said.

I responded, you are right but this morning, you are not going to buy anything from there or eat from there. Come with me, I will make you eat in a comfortable place today.

Her face became downcast because I refused her request of eating in the street. She grudgingly followed me. One of our sons, Tresor was on his Easter holidays and held my hand tightly, because he knows I've always provided them, precious and tasteful surprises that can leave them with good memories. So, he didn't bother like the mum missing her former practice.

As soon as we arrived at the reception of the clinic, we entered the lift. A secretary to the clinic's pediatrician, Dr. JOUBAILY Hussein, entered the lift with us and hit floor 7, I hit floor 6. I asked in surprise to break the ice. Oh! There is now a 7th floor? She answered me, there has always been in this clinic, the 7th floor.

However, to proof myself right I responded that, yes – there has always been that floor, but was called: 'la terrace" or the restaurant of the clinic. And the former lift could not take people there. You have to choose the 6th floor and once there, you can now walk your way to the terrace or 7th floor.

Affirmative, she responded to what I said. We all moved on the supposed 7th floor. As soon as we arrived there I sat my small family – my wife, Rose and son, Tresor. Then, I moved to the waitress to ask the details of how to get a continental breakfast of a middle class family.

Quickly she pulled out the menu à la Carte and I chose the first layer, because it was within our range. I mean, I could afford that and the overall cost of the breakfast for the two, was 4,000 francs CFA.

During the process of getting them the breakfast, I observed that my wife was not too keen to this of my proposal. She shrugged: "A 1,000 francs could have gotten us great breakfast and we could save cost."

I quickly interrupted her. We are not paying for the food or breakfast alone, but the experience and the environment and its whole vicinity.

I spent the day, contemplating and processing the act, which I didn't consider disgusting, however, it needed serious attention and if possible an immediate correction.

She didn't eat the breakfast with a heart of gratitude, but rather intense rage.

While I went through the day, a biblical verse came to mind in order for me to handle the situation once I get home that day, which I did. I successfully handled the situation tactfully, which never triggered any intense argument from her part, but rather intently listened to all the reproaches and concluded into progress advice to see herself henceforth as a middle class citizen of the world for now, the stages can change as life goes on. But, please STOP seeing yourself as a poor woman.

Poverty is a mindset. We are not going to eat there often. Just see, one of our practices, every 31st December for the past few years, as soon as we leave church and on our way home, in the new year festivity, we have been buying for ourselves a good pizza to celebrate the new year, right? She responded, affirmative so, this is how life is as of now, here ends your street dining lifestyle. No more, will you be allowed to eat in the street.

You know what? Leave that life to the average people to do so, but not you again, please. As usual, she told me, I heard you and will do. I know very well, she will do.

Are you ready to face the REALITY?

Over the years, I have on a personal note seen things that if care was not considered or taken appropriately; there are going to be serious problems. I'm not saying that they wouldn't have occurred, but it could have been avoided properly instead of rushing to fix the broken pieces.

One of the mechanics who used to repair one of my vehicles saw his environment taken by the owner of the area (land) in just one day. Himself and his fellow mechanics were forced to go in search of a place to do their mechanic works.

Didn't they see it coming? Or, let me put it this way, were they not informed to clear out in order for the owner to come and take over his land? Yes. They were informed but they did not have the details of when will that happen. The notice was ignored and they moved on with their lives anyway. They thought that they will not be moved out anytime soon, but it will take a while.

Since then, where he now moved to set up his workshop has two key problems.

1. There is lack of a telephone coverage, wherein the poor network, limits him to receive calls on his phone so

that he can direct his old customers to the new found place. This issue has become a strong stumbling block to get all his customers to that place.

2. To get to this new place, there is a strong detour to cover, which for any busy person that does not have time by his side will not be encouraged to go there.

Honesty is a key in any relationship. Always try to be honest in what you do because you never know who may be observing you. This is how my blind trusted mechanic was spotted by my wife, Rose. After her observations, she moved to tell me, *"Honey, won't you mind trying another mechanic and see the difference?"*

First, I ignored her, but patiently she kept insisting for me to just give it a try and see if it does not work, I can go back and stick with my trusted mechanic. I finally gave in to her persistent widow plight for justice as seen in the Holy Bible.

Oh no! It's then I discovered how much I've been duped by this gentle looking but dubious mechanic for close to two years. Since that day onward I have trusted mechanic but always verify their trustworthiness. I have changed him and look for another one since. However, I discovered the same stance that the former one used against me has started visiting the new one's mindset, which will also make me to change this new one as well.

The above scenario has had its recurrence with many mechanics and other service providers. Didn't they see it coming or were they not informed about the pending changes ahead of them? Another one that also suffered from the same scene as mentioned above with my former mechanic is the tire repairer just adjacent to Auchan Ouakam in one of these intercessions.

They have a 24/7 repair service – one in the day, another in the night. Every time, your car has a tire problem they are there to fix the problem and you can safely drive your way to your destination. They too, the spot they were using for their business, has been demanded of them. They are known on that spot, and cannot imagine themselves been asked to leave that place. Time will tell us soon.

Why do we sometimes refuse reality?

This is the scene for mechanic of all types, but sometimes, we forget to know that we are all service providers regardless the service. We are all businessmen, so let's learn to renew our mindsets daily.

Chapter Eight

Good Habits

The Power of Good Habits

You are what you are, all due to what you think whole day – Zig Zigla.

I never knew that commitment can obviously make you start a project, but it takes consistency to carry on or bring it to a finishing table. Hence, in your habit development, what requires your commitment and what requires your amendment to better streamline it for success? If you choose to avoid, it is good, however, that choice ought to weigh the pros and cons to see if it is not the opposite or a good side of it.

I did struggle to begin this chapter, especially with the challenges of meeting other people's needs that they cannot stop disturbing me for their own projects to be taken care of. Welcome to the selfish world. It is where, people will first think of themselves; then, later on – others' right or privilege might likely come in if need be.

Whenever I thought of good habits, there is one key word that comes to mind. It is *OBEDIENCE*. *Good habits get their power supply from consistent or committed obedience and nothing less.*

It took the Israelites 40 years for them to cross the Jordan River. A three-day distance journey all the headaches they went through in the desert were due to their disobedience. So to frame it in this format any time, there is a bad habit, remember, if there is no element of disobedience in the scene.

There is even a scientific law to that effect. It is called the Newton 3rd law of motion: *"To every action, there is always equal and opposite reaction."* If you do what is good; it is good that will follow you. Jesus Christ did provide a recipe of a peaceful living in our communities, but we struggle with that, because we are not willing to adhere to the provided principles of good living. Isn't that amazing?

Bad habits gets easily incorporated into our lives, but to let them off from our midst, it becomes a serious challenge. So, be watchful, in your dealings and be willing to learn how to undo certain things that you may have once considered to be good habits.

One afternoon while taking lunch with my small family, a discussion emerged and all of the sudden, I mentioned cassette. We used to have cassettes ranging from 45 minutes, 60 minutes to 90 minutes recorder. One of our sons is talkative and very irritating. As if he is running a talking competition. See, anything of value will obviously require proper taming. We, as parents, are currently working on that to tame this handsome young man to reduce his plenty talking to essential ones.

So, I shouted on him; Hey! C-90 then his elder brother asked: What is C-90? It is a cassette that used to have a recording capacity of 90 minutes. However, the message was not still clear to him, because he does not know the meaning of cassette.

Well, I visited our grandfather, Google, to help me make my sons understand what I mean. It was understood and then we moved on. It is how the good memory of cassette and what they have done for some of us during those times. Today, cassettes' presence in any concert is not really relevant. They have become obsolete.

Just the same way cassettes used to be important to the previous generation and brought music to them, but today they are obsolete and of no use, it is the same with some habits, they have become obsolete. Sometimes this habits expire without us knowing, it is important for us to know when to let go and when to hold on. If you have any habit that looks like a cassette, please throw it away, because it will not serve any good purpose today.

For some of us that are computer literate. There was also another piece of object called: Floppy disk or in short, a diskette. This was where information in files form like the one I am currently typing were stored for future use or to be transferred into another computer or still, be accessed if need be. In fact, they were so good in getting us organized or put all electronic files in one place and can later return to them and access the stored information with no headache. This too, has become obsolete. In fact, they were as good as an object to a certain level. They became personified to use on very beautiful girls in every society. We used to call those beautiful girls, Diskette, like what is seen today in current expression, WhatsApp girl! It was gorgeous. So, if you have a habit today, that resembled a diskette, please it is no longer useful neither for you nor anyone in your current environment. You ought to know what you DO NOT want in order for you to look for what you really want.

Great is thy faithfulness! Is a very good hymn in one of these Baptist hymns books? Gorgeous! Many good habits yesterday were very great in serving our needs, but as time went by they become obsolete. We can no longer think of using them, lest we will be ridiculed as to why we are so old school. Hence, to avoid such stance in our future endeavors, we need to learn and unlearn certain things in order to move forward in life. Certain habits maybe great today for a reason, but be watchful for the day they can become a crime and you become a victim.

Let me give you a personal anecdote: I became a procurement assistant in June 2011, since then, I have been sending out the RFQ (Request For Quotations) and my line manager had no problem for me sending them out to suppliers, service providers, etc. Until, September 2017, it became an insult to authority (my line manager). I was queried for doing so. Astounded by the query, I responded but sir, I have been doing this with no problem all these years, why today you now see it as a crime? All I got was this: *I keep on telling you that what you were doing was not professional, but you ignored me to a point I have to query you before you can realize that it is not appropriate.* The rest is history. I had good intention about the act of sending out of RFQ, but it has become obsolete — a diskette or a cassette in our procurement unit. It is no longer useful.

This is how in most relationship, people or couple for some reasons, hold on the yesterday practices that brought about their partners. All of the sudden, either one of the partners, now no longer see that practice as his/her own cup of tea (he/she does not like it). Folks know your partner and also learn to undo certain things that have become obsolete.

Even the world or universe that we are in is not stagnant. We wake up from our slumber, depending on your own personal schedule or set an alarm, 6:00am or

7:00am. Before, it is 8:00am, we see the sun raising from the East and we now know it very well, that sun, you saw raising from the East is going to set in the West side of your area. If that scenario is adjustable, why not contemplate on adjusting your habits as well?

One of female family friends, whose name I am not going to mention here for some reasons. She was sacked from her job for a reason, after she has shared with us. I stared at my wife, and we did discuss something through our eye contacts concerning her. However, we could not rebuke her because it was no longer useful to make any correction at that time. Once we left her home; I quickly asked my wife, Rose. What your friend shared with us. Was she right to behave that way? My wife said: *Hell NO!* It is not about what you know and how you have been doing it, she should have just considered the boss' request as an order and it could have saved her from the imminent layoff with immediate effect.

Sometimes, what is required of us is to consider a gentle request as an order and move on and do it in order for us to have our peace of mind; not to claim a right, which is so flimsy and knowing our modern society, can become a scheme of layoff.

I was once opportune to watch one of Jack Ma's small, but very educative video clips on YouTube, he said: *"Life is lived by stages, when you are younger, let's say between the ages of 15 through 25 years of age, make a lot of mistakes and learn from them. From the ages 25 through 35, start turning your errors into solution finding. However, from 35 through 40, be very careful in making mistakes, because they can cost you a lot."*

This did not make much sense to me by then, until I started processing what has been said and how to get this incorporated into my personal life as a lesson. I have come to notice that it is also a mindset. Whenever, I hear that there was a police outrageous act on black communities in USA. I cannot stop to wonder. Yet, there is a huge amount of African brothers and sisters, who will even sell their plots of land, houses, in order to go to the USA.

There is a game; I like to play with my wife, Rose. It was very good when we started our relationship. However, after two years into our marriage, she no longer sees the use of playing this game. I kept requesting for us, from time to time, engage ourselves into playing this game. All I get from her was a no. Whenever I asked the reason to her refusal, this is what I get, "You don't know how to play it well." Then, one evening, I requested for her to teach me the way, she wants us to play that game. She sent me to consult our current grandfather, Google. She said, "Google it, maybe you might learn some good lessons from your research and know how to play the game right or to my taste."

This brought in the phrase: Let Go!

Have you ever engaged into something very important for you, but the odds for you to achieve that thing are currently higher than you can imagine?

Let me give you a personal scenario. On the 6th of September 2016 – my divorce case at the Senegalese tribunal got its temporary pronouncement. Where the judge of the case temporarily pronounced us divorced, before the final verdict a scene that didn't go down well with my now ex-wife.

Know this, there are people in your life that are there temporary. You need to have the 4-key in order to detect first and then know how to handle them scrupulously.

Four keys in this scene are:
Wisdom

Knowledge

Understanding

Discernment.

Without them in your personal life, I am not saying that you cannot make it in life, but it will a very slim success. If you do succeed, it will never last.

Those who have these four keys in their good habits development system, even if they lost all their fortune, in no time, can gain everything they have lost. In fact, failure is a tangible stepping-stone to better success.

The academic school year 2016/2017 was about to start. So, while I was in hospital, recuperating from the injuries sustained from my now ex. I started reflecting on what can go wrong, if I am not around.

I sent a WhatsApp message to my now ex-pastor, because I know he still have influence over my now-ex to convince her in giving me the boy, Ebenezer so that I can help in his proper education.

A request that was seen by this pastor as an insult to humanity, we had a much tensioned debate on the matter and my divorce stance. Sometimes, people will tell you manage (bear), but if it is their turn for them to manage, they cannot afford to do so. Be very vigilant about where your pieces of advice are coming from. When you are in a serious mess, you will be surprised that nobody will come to your aid. So, get wisdom in your dealings.

Desperate not to see this boy spoiled like it is the case of his elder sisters. I shared the concern with one of my colleagues, Joseph Kwuana who has traversed two kinds of divorces and also have children in the process. With such stance in relationship, what is required of a man to do? I posed the question.

He responded: Let go!

Let go! I exclaimed. Are you kidding me? Have you thought of the boy's sanity or care, even his education?

See, they know that taking the boy from you will cause you to reconsider your divorce decision and because you will not want the boy to suffer. You may likely renounce your divorce decision and continue to live a miserable life just because you want to protect a young lad. You need to get matured in this. So, relax. That boy will come back to you whether they like it or not. He prophesied that day to heal my unbelief and then, I relaxed.

Tough it could be, I swallowed my pride and allow time to take its tour on the life of Ebenezer. I let go!

From that day, 6th up to 21st of September 2016, school was in session, but Ebenezer was not taken to school. The school authority issued a concern notice to me, which I took to my lawyer.

Finally, she took the boy to school. Then, life started becoming unbearable for both the boy and the mom, because if I am not around, taking the boy to school is a REAL headache for her.

In October 2016, complains started raining concerning the boy's lack of concentration in class. Not doing his assignments, etc. She now wanted me to step in to take the boy, but it never amounted to much. Because my lawyer told me, she has to write renouncing the custody. To which, she refused to do.

We entered into another month, November 2016 — where the complaints about the boy could not stop raining. Then, another colleague — Bacuya Senesi, who was or has been playing a double standard between us intervened and requested that I reconsider my decision to take the boy because he is suffering and lacks the necessary things a child should have for his schooling. He wanted, through the process, the mom could seize that opportunity to come back to my bosom. Little did he know whom, really Comrade Fayiah LEIBA is.

I stepped in against my lawyer's will to pick the boy without proper documentation between us because she is the one that the court gave the custody. Since then, the 21st November 2016 to date, the boy, though legally, he is supposed to be with the mum according to the court's pronouncement on 6th December 2017, he is with me to date. Isn't letting go quiet OK?

There are battles that never needed your physical action in them, just let go. If you let go, and pray about it, the long awaited breakthrough will come back to you when you least expected it.

I have been criticized a lot, for loving a devil, according to my critics. President Donald J. Trump, the 45th president of the USA, unlike Barrack Obama, has more critics than praise singers.

One thing the critical world on Trump, failed to note is this. Trump is not a politician. He is straightforward person instead. He is not a conformist. He does not watch his tune of language when it is time to express the truth.

On several occasions, I have been into serious debates because I love Trump. I have explained my stance. In fact, the more I keep explaining things to some of Trump's critics to look at him with another or a neutral eye or still, focus their attention on the good side of him. They see nothing good about him, but the devil in human clothing.

To a point, as of this day, 3rd April 2018, I have chosen to let go as well or completely ignored any argument concerning Trump. After all, after his presidency, he will still be a businessman and never a politician.

Not only this, I am 40+, reflecting on Jack Ma's life stage description, I chose this year 2018, a year of PEACE as my personal resolution. In my office, most colleagues want my old Comrade Fayiah LEBA, wherein; I will say the truth come what may.

Over the years, I have realized what I have thus far gotten from most of these actions. Are they worth the cost? So, I chose to let go the unnecessary argument as well.

In fact, this has been accredited to my wife, Rose. Since I remarried, I have become totally a new person. She gets the credit. One day, she told me: *"They really don't know you too well. For you are somebody that can decide to refrain from something or a habit — whether good or bad. You start the count down, up to 21 days; you have completely changed to a new person. I have seen that in you. You have been with them, for the 12 years, yet, they don't know this about you?"*

Maybe, some may know it. One thing I am sure of is that I believe in personal character development on a daily basis. As the clever saying goes: **"You cannot remain the same"** Meaning: You are bound to change, regardless your character." Is Robert Mugabe still the president of Zimbabwe? Not at all! Is Yayah Jammeh still the president of The Gambia? Lie! Lie! He is not. So, instead of letting situation to change you, change your situation. It is far better if you have a bad habit and you are not aware of it, watch out the comments of people about you, and make amendments. Don't be a stumbling block to your progress for life is so short to give in your possession and regret later on.

Remember this, you will never live for 100 years. If you do, it will be with serious pain in the body. Don't waste your youthful years, invest them and harvest later. Good habits can be cultivated.

It is just a matter of 21 days. A three-week period to learn a new, but a good habit and be watchful of your environment as well. Bear in mind, that what is good today for such and such environment can become a serious crime later. Remember the cassette and diskette scenario I shared earlier and know that sometimes, the good habits can be nuisance to your progress tomorrow. Did I say, after some years? No! I said, tomorrow. It has happened to me. You can be the next victim, if you are not careful with the way, you handle things in life.

Is every advice a good advice?

Yes. However, it depends on the context, environment (soil) or the event.

I hear people say, be careful whom you take your advice from. If the context, the soil is good, the advice will be fruitful regardless of whom it is coming from.

The hard work is now for you and I to know when and where such piece of advice is appropriate to implement in order for the dished out advice to become useful.

It takes a great number of personal efforts for such schemes to work

On this fine day, let me put this straight. All days are very fine depending on the circumstances at stake. And you know why they are all fine, because they are all created equal in God's sight.

As usual, my wife suggested that I shop for fish for the remaining days of the month of May 2018. It was the 10th May 2018.

Senegal, my resident nation, duty station, is a Muslim dominated nation. However, since she got her independence from the former colonial power, France. She kept all her oriented colonial public holidays intact. This day was a public holiday for both the white and blue-collar workers. But petty trading was not the case, so I went to shop for fish on Thursday, when it was supposed to be done on weekends. This piece of advice came from my wife, Rose.

Let me show you the reason behind this advice. One of our sons was due for Cambridge English test on Saturday 12th May 2018 and arrival at the venue was scheduled at 7:20am. Not to disrupt it with any of our established daily activity, she came up with the suggested advice, which I found it to be in place.

When I reached at my usual venue in Yara Kapa to shop for fish, this is one of the beaches in Bel Air. I spotted Awa Ndiaye, one of the women that clean the bought fish for me. Client! Today, I will work with you to buy fish. She exclaimed in Wolof.

Usually, I've refused such offers to assist me, because sometimes instead of helping you, as a foreigner, she will form a coup d'état against you (foreigner) to dupe you profusely.

Let me give you a piece of advice here. Any environment you found yourself in future, please endeavor to learn the common local language(s). I have come to realize that it helps a lot. In fact, it is the scheme of a near culture.

I started asking for the price of the set of fish and after few discussions, I will tell Awa Ndiaye for us to move on. After we moved on; I asked her, if the quoted last price is OK from the look of things. Yes, she confidently answered. This gave me the courage to go back and buy that set of fish, then another and the third and last set. It is OK for the month.

This scheme was learnt from one of the chapters of the book *"How I Raised Myself from Failure to Success"* *by Frank Bettger* which I got the title from another book *The Secrets of Closing the Sale by Zig Ziglar and Tom Ziglar*. People will want to help if someone closer to them is serving in your favor as an intermediary person. It stands like this – the one that knows the culture will speak better to the locals in your favor to his/her people. In fact, s/he is better understood than you. Even if you know the language, this scene of letting the local person as either a guide for you is called near–culture scheme.

Sometimes, it is better to use than depending on your own scheme. I have used wherever I sense the need.

"The wall is down, but you have to climb over the rubble." – T.D. Jakes.

I was in a visitors' toilet one afternoon and the same time, scrolling through my Facebook app on my iPhone where I spotted the above–mentioned. It has other detailed explanations, which ranged from this stage.

When you sign a contract, there are always contingency clauses anyone of us in that identical contract needs to be aware of. If I willed my sons few houses but I said they had to be married and above 21 years of age to get them, that's a contingency clause. There are specific things that make you eligible to receive what is in contracting relation. The wall is down, God already took care of that part; the contingency clause is you have to climb over the rubble. You need to do something about the challenges at stake. It's not enough for God to just bring the wall down if you're not going to rise above the rubble. God has equipped you to conquer the opinions of others, as well as the insecurities that reside within you. This is your week to climb over the remnants of the wall God brought down to walk into the Promised Land! - Rev. T. D. Jakes.

Chapter Nine

Self Confidence

"A little drop of water makes a mighty ocean." Julia Abigail Fletcher Carney

We all know that courage is like a little drop of water adage, which goes like this. ***"A little drop of water makes a mighty ocean."*** Small courageous steps, once they are regularly carried out can be turned into what is called: Confidence. We all need the fuel of courage to overcome or undertake any challenge in our respective lives.

This is how Esther, a young Jewish girl whose uncle Mordecai trained, she was an orphan. Due to their precarious lifestyle, the uncle Mordecai was not also an easy fellow to live with in terms of discipline.

Let me share with you an anecdote I once experience with a colleague of mine. There was this early morning after having arrived in the office. She called in an alarming manner. Comrade! Come, oh! Come! I don't know what people see in this office, she lamented. She shared with me an appalling mail she received from one of her colleagues.

In my usual stance to calm her down and tell her to keep a low profile. I gave her a story of Joseph in the Bible to make her see that suffering is actually part of life. In fact, without it there is no concrete or tangible progress in this thing called life. I went on by saying to her. Show me in the whole world, where have you someone who has made a great name, such as Nelson Mandela, and the like that never went through a great challenge in their lives as individuals.

They never invited themselves into a pity party because if you invite yourself into a pity party, then, be rest assured that it is a party and you will be alone with no one by your side to help celebrate with you. This is because, while you will be crying "why me", others will be removing dust off their clothes and move on with life. They will be making breakthrough in no time, when you will be pity parting alone with no one around to help you.

So consider it pure joy whenever you face trials of many kinds. In fact, today the media it being general news, TV, radio, etc., any good news is not news that sells. However, ugly news such as catastrophes is the good one that will require proper attention to the general public. If only, our continual courage can be stepped up into publicizing good news instead. These courageous scenes would have developed into a serious confidence.

Learn to distinguish yourself by becoming a disciple of good news carrier. Remember, a little drop of water can be turned into a mighty ocean. Your courageous steps can be turned into a serious confidence, which if properly channeled, can become a success in no time. Note this, there are four secrets in doing so. This is the kind of confidence that was built in the life of a young Jewish girl, Esther when she was trained by a kind of man of his word, his uncle, Mordecai. He was not an easy person to live by. As some of us may be aware that to turn a piece of gold into whatever design we want it to be turned into; we first ought to get the goldsmith. Who, in return will take the gold through the necessary processes in order to make the required design. You and I, will need a refining fire to chip off the negative scenes of our respective lives, and once the dirt are taken from us, what remains will be the required pure gold we want for our lives.

Here are the four secrets.

Having self-control over your heart.

If you ever are going to make headway in anything in life, you ought to have self-control, not only for it to be rooted into your heard as mentioned above, but in life generally speaking. It must be something like, Take it or leave it scenario. This does not happen to self-pity people at all. It is for the courageous ones, which is not easy, because we will face difficulties in life.

There was a time when we went on an appointment. We arrived on time, but due to the traffic jams in most cities across the world, the person who gave us the appointment and said, a minute later, we will not be received. Obviously, we were on time, but the person in question came late. At least, 20 minutes later. In the meantime, whilst you wait for either an opportunity or to receive a message from either your superior and high personality. If the waiting is not forthcoming, what should be our attitude toward the wait? Most of us, would have lost our patience and start to whine before the supposed boss stepped in. Once he sees us, our countenance will manifest our impatience. It will be evident that we are not happy with what he has done by telling us to be on time and then he is late, he will now be the one humbly requesting for forgiveness. Do you know that sometimes, our supposed bosses, even if they are wrong in their acts, can refuse to acknowledge it and in such stance, we ought have self-control lest our right become an insult to our supposed bosses, if the manner which we show our dissatisfaction is inappropriate.

Imagining you are in a strange environment.

Let's say you are a foreigner and your supposed boss happens to be the citizen of the land. If that kind of a person is a quick-tempered in his own home country and he wrongs you. Will you keep a low profile in that situation or you will tell him your piece of mind? A question with a twofold answers:

1. Say your piece of mind and you lose the job;

2. Or remain silent and wave the scene in order for you to keep your job.

I have always told people and this include myself as well. Nobody can make you angry without your consent. Or, let me put it in this way: it is the boiling anger in your life which is there waiting for you to be ignited and bang! You will burst open and you will vent to your displeasure. However, in your anger, please do not say something that you will regret later on. So, to avoid such atmospheres, remain silent in the process. Time is the greatest healer in God's own timing. Give the situation a timeframe; you will be relieved from such pain in no time. Whilst you wait, beware of your attitude as well, for manners make a man.

Nobody wishes for evil in his or her life. It is allowed, maybe to strengthen us. In the process, mind your attitude and actions, in any form. They can be difficult, but watch them kindly. If at all the evil knocks at your doorpost, beware of your actions or reactions. Most often, husbands – who go through challenges in their work places, once they get home, their office angers, are dished out to the family at home. It takes an understanding wife, to console the wounded heart of the heart of the concerned husband to reframe from dishing his anger on either the innocent wife or the children.

Let's be very watchful to our actions when occurred somewhere should not be spilled over to other people that were not present on the scene where the misfortune presented itself. Strange environments are everywhere in life, it depends on how you manage them. Manage them well and don't let them spill over in order not to let the disturbing situation to escalate to where it was not supposed to reach. Be warned.

Do you know how to forgive and forget?

Forgiveness is a process. Just for me to secure an expression which might one day serve a key purpose in my life or the life of another human being, I wrote this story. The expression is this one: double-take look

This one is achieved. How do you know it? I have been observant at the reactions of my wife, Rose towards sexually related things. To a point, I began to question internally whether she really loves me. Upbringing is really hardcore in some societies. Her tune of voice is fourfold:
   a) When she likes things or something is in her favor;
   b) When she is convinced about something;
   c) When she is in for something and then all of the sudden, the opposite of that presents itself;
   d) When the unexpected wrong takes place. It is where she cannot control her emotions.

We all know that when someone likes something and it is presented to him or her. Gracious God. They will cherish it with all their heart, soul and mind. However, if the opposite is in sight, the reaction is not funny.

The second one, when she is convinced about something, obviously she is very much easy going and trust my words, you will love to be in her company, because you will really see the better part of her.

Unfortunately, the last two ones are the greatest concerns of her life that required huge amendment. If her life, were a nation that just gained independence, then the constitution ought to be rewritten in order for the actions in building up the nation can be geared to a worthy cause. And if need be, those who fought that independence, will ought to either be an observer sit or counseling sit and be called upon if there is a need for their counseling in running of the nation.

See. There is a general belief that those who for the independence of any society are not supposed to be the one in power of that nation in question. They are like military scenes in dealing with the affairs of the fragile nation. Hence, giving them the seat of power will not properly help in the nation building of this identified fragile nation. Why? The reason being, not everyone has undergone through military training. They will bring a discipline that will not suit the society they are given to govern. Anarchy will set in. This is where the unexpected things or wrong things take place. This is the place where the freedom fighters yesterday cannot control themselves, because they would, in their own mind say, "do you know how much we fought for this nation to be protected or be delivered from the hands of our colonizers?"

You know, every society has its own regulatory stance. Many a time we think that what worked yesterday in society can be blanket stance for everything in life. It is a wrong self-confidence mindset and we have to be very careful, otherwise, we will be doing more harm than good.

One fine night, after having gone through our regular night devotions.
General evening devotion with our lovely boys, who are in fact, the reason I am writing down this short story due to their immense efforts in getting the required discipline so that they can become good citizens of any society they found themselves tomorrow.

As devout couple in Christ Jesus, after the children are sent to bed and we are now alone to ourselves, we moved on to read the Holy Word (the Bible). Note this, my wife, Rose for wisdom gaining, reads the book of Proverbs and then I read a chapter of a book daily. We are not bothered how long it will take us, because it is our supper and we are supposed to eat our spiritual food. Why won't we prosper or have peace of mind as a couple? Because, Jesus Christ is the centered of our relationship; does anyone see something wrong about that?

She was barely seven weeks pregnant with our son. *"Honey, Pastor Bradford called me today, and shared with me that since I am now pregnant I should stop having sex".* I gave her a double-take look and kept quiet for a very long time till I even felt asleep.

In the course of reading and listening to a library of 530 books as I write this story. To be precise 8th May 2018 I have developed a Christ-driven attitude in dealing with difficult situation particularly the scenes that present accusations leveled against me.

Some of us may be aware of the story of the woman caught in committing adultery and the scribes of the law brought her before the Lord Jesus Christ. According to them, the Law of Moses commanded them to have her stoned to dead, because it is insanity to allow her live amongst them. Jesus Christ in His omnipresence wisdom bent his head down and started writing in the ground. They all left the scene one after the other and left the woman alone with Him. After a long while, He rose up his head and saw no one and then asked the woman. Woman, where are your accusers? She responded, "They have left". He responded to her, "Go and sin no more".

Every time, I am accused of something, instead of reacting or even answering to the person accusing me, I take it into the scene, I call: PROCESS. It depends to the feelings, sometimes, the processing scene, can be an hour or two. Sometimes, a week or a month, however, most often it gets into years analyzing the whole scenario to better know what to either answer or relate concerning that scene.

Processing has become part and parcel of my current daily life. In fact, it is the self-confidence every one of us should be eager to acquire for any good breakthrough in life. And guess what? It is getting better on a daily basis. In case, I even forget about them and allow time to serve as the Judge of the issue at stake.

But let me tell you this. It is not easy to **be a process-driven person**. It is very costly sometimes. I do react sometimes, because I am human and entitled to few errors. However, every time, the ugly side of me wants to gain its absolute power. I call my name: Comrade Fayiah LEIBA! Please learn to process things. It is far better than engaging yourself into bitter arguments when the person – all they want is to see you disgraced. Can't you see the writing on the wall? I humbly bow down into process scene. In fact, I have on personal note found much and better peace with it thus far.

However, whenever you engaged yourself into processing things. Refrain from keeping stock of wrongs the person(s) has or might have done to you. If you don't refrain from doing so, this is what will happen to you like it is seen in this anecdote of an angry snake below. A story is told of a scrolling snake that was passing by a standing saw – head sank in the soil and the handle up. *"A snake in a carpentry shop hurt itself a little as it crawled over a saw. The snake turned and bit the saw, which hurt him badly in his mouth. Not understanding what was happening to it and thinking the saw was attacking him, the snake rolled around the saw to suffocate it with all of its strength.*

The snake was killed because he wouldn't release the saw. You read this text, you sometimes react in anger, wanting to hurt the ones who hurt you, but end up hurting yourself more than them. In life, it may be better to either ignore or process people's acts, situations, and the pains you are not willing to let go. The consequences of holding on to that pain will often cause irreversible stress and continue to hurt you in the future".

Any time, you are faced with an unforgiving mindset. Take it to the factory and process it. Once you are done, you will see yourself as a new person. Remember, forgiveness is a process.

The respect for authority

Don't expose your dirty laundries.
One of the challenges we all face in life is trying to look good before people and let the other person looks bad before others. I was once opportune in discussing with one of my colleagues concerning the maltreatments some of us go through in the office. The persistent injustice leveled against some of us. I could not hold it but to expose the practice, but my colleague saw this habit that was controlling my behaviors as a sign of lack of discipline.

She was a conformist by nature, and due to her conformist state of mind, she gets unmerited favors (grace). That's why she is criticizing some of us that have been tortured for failing to conform to the norms (the status quo). I have the urge to mention her name, but not wanting to face lawsuit, I will refrain from mentioning her name instead. So I will label the conversation between the person and I in coded language, which means you have to have worked in my office, BACOCO for a long period of time particularly during these years: 2006 through 2018 to be able to detect who I had that conversation with me.

XY: Comrade! You are a nuisance fellow – do you know that?

Me: Well, sometimes it requires that to get things done the right way.

XY: What things do you want to be done the right way?

I started elaborating a long list of things that were going on in our office that needed to be done the right way, but unfortunately, those in authority, due to their selfish stance or superiority mindset; they marginalized good measures that are meant for the common good of everyone. So, in order to let them know my displeasure, I have to behave that way. Who knows, it might change to the better way.

XY: Don't expose your dirty laundries! There is no need for you to behave the way you think; it is not the right way. For there are principles, abide by them, period!

I just keep quiet and move away from her, because she was not speaking in my favor but in the favor of the oppressors and never the oppressed.

Hey! Be very careful when you think that you have been marginalized. You may be doing yourself more harm than good. Society rewards those who conform to the norms and not waywardness. Who amongst you, will want to have a wayward child? None! So, why do you choose to be wayward? It almost took me a decade long interval to come to my senses and decided to change for a common good.

However, these were the two fold senses I gained over that long period of time to stay in that state of mind – *you do me, I do you syndrome*. the bad lessons and the good lessons. Let me start with the bad lessons. From 2009 to December 2017 I really suffered moral, mental, and physical tortures from those who were supposed to protect me. For them, I was not a conformist, so the best way to handle me was to torture me strongly in order for them to humble me. I have always told people this clever saying that I think, I must have gathered it from the Holy Bible. *"No two WRONGS can make one right."* But to be frank, I didn't understand the meaning truly. I did use it anyway. Let me give you some analysis on how I now understand the above boldfaced and italic statement. Use Christ's piece of advice. *If someone slaps you on one chick, turn him the other chick to slap as well.* Can you make it? With the help of the Almighty God in your midst, it is possible. The bad torture lessons, instead of getting into a pity party where as we all know it leave you alone, I chose to rather be strong and learn to exploit the difficult lessons in my favor instead.

The good lessons extirpated from the bad ones. They helped me become a better person. In fact, it has always made me to reflect on the story of Joseph in the cleverest book, the Bible. Joseph mother, Rachel was the love of his father (Jacob), who stole the blessings of his brother, Esau. Sometimes, I get confused for no reason. How can a loving God cherish a thief? Then after profound reflection, I condemned myself for thinking that way. Are you that pure or just, Comrade? Not at all, I have my own flaws as well. Joseph was the first born to Rachel and his junior brother, Benjamin.

Women, this is for you. Make sure your husband loves you a lot regardless. You have that power; however, if you lose that grip off your hand, you will never get it again. I can remember sharing this from my 19-year failed marital life experience, a story of how most women lose the grip of the love of their lives due to little negligence. You see, life has its own surprises. We ought to be very careful. Whenever a young man meets a young woman and they start their dating process. Love has its apex. As years flow and time passes, the climax of the love is set to dwindle. What keeps the two persons together is their individual commitment to each. A little negligence will end in catastrophic scene, which no one would like.

Especially, the arrival of children to most couples is considered to be the most joyous lifestyle for the two. Just wait for a few years when the children become the attention seekers in your midst; it is the starting point from stages such as toddlers through teenagers. This is where the love of the mother of the house starts to shift from the husband to the children. In her mind, the children will take care of her, if at all the husband is to derail in the nearest future. This care taking can only take place if the supposed children are well trained educationally in the first place. If it is not so, then, you will be buried miserably. Or, your church (any community you belong to) might better handle your funeral whilst you will be resting in peace. This too, provided you were actually a committed member.

So, to avoid these setbacks, why not you consider handling your soul partner with fear and trembling?

Passive Indifference.

Whenever you get used to something, someone, or a work place - there are tendencies that sometimes, we take that life for granted. It is human. This is where, every one of us are supposed to be careful. Take a look on this anecdote. When someone applies for a job vacancy, He is so keen in getting that job. He is always grateful to God for blessing him with the job. It is like learning a new skill. As soon as we mastered the skill that we can now do things, without any second thought we tend to relax. Then, we start receiving gentle reproaches, which if we are careful, can help us improve either the relationship or interpersonal the more, however, if pride sets in, then we have to be careful. Why? Because at this stage, we will think, not only we have mastered the work at hand, but we will start to think that we are even more qualified than the job we are given to do. This is the time, we just do what we are asked to do, and refuse to go the extra mile like we used to do previously. Negligence from any gesture or sign can be shown clearly.

This too, can happen between couples. Irons sharpen irons. As soon as we start to observe frictions in order for every one of us to better know our respective right positions in that relationship or environment. I don't take nonsense. The nonsense you may not be willing to take, is considered as a motivation sign for another person.

Couples! Let us be observant in actions that come our way. Not this. Any time, your partner, a colleague, a best friend goes out of his/her way to do something for you. Don't take it for granted. S/He expects a return, it might not be the same as what s/he must have offered, but a replica will be OK. It is better to give than to receive. Because once you receive, you ought to pay back Don't neglect the gesture by saying it is normal for him/her to do so. Consider it a debt. In so doing, you will have a balanced life.

Chapter | Ten

The Grace of God

Only the grace of God can change your lives as individuals

I was reading a book entitled: L'Accroissement Limite written by Pastor Felix Birama Ndiaye. I was on chapter 2 of his book and he was talking about the grace of

God the paragraph that spoke of the lilies of the field and King Solomon's garments.

The comparison between a university graduate and a primary school leaver is if we are opportune to see the primary school leaver in a Director General's position. The only thing we can base our argument upon is the grace of God. However, those with bad intentions, will say, he must have played a strong politic to get there without noticing the hand of God in the scene.

Across other paragraphs, he also spoke of the grace that was accorded to Joseph to become the Prime Minister of Egypt. A scene, many cannot relate to it because he was not a citizen of this nation only God's grace that can trigger such blessings into his arms.

Then, I thought of President George M. Weah of Liberia. If our arguments are only based on education — he's an underdog for many who may not believe in such special grace coming to an individual like him to become a great nation's president just like that. He beats the well-educated and respected and down to the earth man during their presidential run off.

I was also fortunate to watch an interview, one female journalist asked *Mr. JOSEPH Bockai, why is it that he has to become president before he can achieve the dreams he has for the nation? He responded, when you are not the one in charge, your ideas, regardless how strong vision behind your ideas is, they will be marginalized.*

This gave me a flashback when I used to take initiatives in our procurement unit but because I was not the head of the unit my initiatives were considered insults to authority. In fact, it was considered taking initiatives without any supervisory counsel backing the initiative. It served me as a stumbling block to my progress as a junior staff for close to a decade to be precise from May 2010 through May 2018. Eight years I was locked to the same position, as a procurement assistant without any recommendation for tangible promotion, like it was the case with other colleagues, whom we considered yes-men, yet they got promoted and we, that thought we know it all, were ignored.

Maybe God put me in that seemingly God forsaken position to teach me a lesson, which in fact, has served as a catalyst to acquiring entrepreneurship knowledge to rather establish a corporate ladder instead of fighting to climb it.

The grace of God has its surprises on mankind. In May 2010, there was an interview conducted in my then office, BACOCO for the position of a Procurement Officer. The candidates to both the test and interview by nationalities were as follow:

a) Gambian, who now happened to be my current Line Manager;

b) Nigerian;

c) Guinean in the person of Rangoubongo Spencer, current Head of Services at the ECOWAS Commission;

d) Bissau Guinean; and

e) A Senegalese.

As we all know, in most businesses today, sometimes interviews are only conducted for formalities, the favorite candidate can be already selected.

Every candidate was given the right computer to work on. That is, a person from a French background was given a desktop computer with an operating system in French and the one with an English background was as well given the machine with an English operating system, except one person, *Mr. Mara Mansaray Sory* – The Gambian candidate.

Mr. Malick Keita, was the one who did the distribution and Mr. *Mara Mansaray Sory* was finding it difficult to work, because both the operating system and the keyboard were in French and he had no French at all.

The Admin Officer who was supposed to invigilate the test, due to other commitments delegated that process to me being one of her subordinate staff in those days.

When Mr. Cham highlighted this faux pas to me, I quickly called Mr. Keita to do something about it so that all participants can be given a fair treatment.

He angrily responded me, which got me angry too and guess what I did. I came in the hall and in my anger, I showed all the difficult steps to Mr. *Mara Mansaray Sory.* The Bible teaches us that in our anger, we should not sin. So, I did the opposite instead. Believe me or not, he excellently passed his test, and graciously, he was able to beat everyone as well at the interview.

At the end of the day, he was the one that was retained for the post. Do you see what the grace of God can do for us? They meant evil for him because his standard in procurement was very much higher. So, if he has failed the test, they would have eliminated him, but unfortunately and to everyone's disappointment he became the Procurement Services.

To date, he has always been marginalized by many colleagues. Some even considered him not only weak, but not supposed to be the Procurement Officer of BACOCO, because for some, he's too dull and not fit for purpose.

My ignorance of God's grace upon the life of certain people has one way or the other made me to look low upon him. This was not done by my own intention, but due to peer pressure or instigations received from mal-intentioned colleagues who used to tell me: "Your boss is useless."

Today, whenever they say this to me, I tell them: No! He's not useless, but very important because if God's grace were not with him, he would not have been a staff of BACOCO, during Dr. Koroma Shellu's regime because he was a very strict leader. He has survived that.

God's grace is like rain water that is required for plants to bear fruits or other plants to provide food for mankind and other animals.

Once there is a drought, the land will not produce food required by mankind to survive.

Many of us are suffering because of the lack of God's grace, which is considered here as the rainy water required for plants to survive in order for other animals to survive too through those plants.

Any time, you found yourself in an environment when others gain unmerited favor. Please don't envy them, ask God to show you what you need to do to reclaim your own rainy water (God's grace).

Jabez's name meant: Pain, yet he requested for his blessings and it was given to him as requested. What are you waiting or holding you back?

I have a theorem, which has worked for me. In 2004, like any other African child, I was very eager to cross the Atlantic Ocean to either go to Europe or America. An African American lady shared a very sad scene; what our mindsets can do for us. She told us that we can remain in Africa achieved great things in life, provided we think that way.

Today, most people prefer to live in Africa than either Europe or America. Yet, most Africans still think that without going there they cannot achieve their dreams.

On the 6th October 2018, a former classmate told me that he has won the DV Program to travel to USA, and what is now holding him, is the ticket money for him and his lovely family.

This is another failed mindset. He thinks going to USA will save him and his family. In fact, he told me that he prefers to be a slave in USA rather than suffer in Africa. He does not even know that God's goodness can be everywhere in this world. All that is required of him is a change in mindset and the grace of God's abundant blessings will be his portion.

Does he know that? Not at all.

In fact, for some, their desire to succeed in life made them to no longer have the fear of God in what they do. Some will even say, it's not that bad inasmuch as I don't have any intention to kill any human being in what I'm doing. Does what you think about daily or to do glorify God? Do you have God's fear in your mind? Without such fear, you will be wasting your precious time trying to succeed in life when His fear is not there for He protects those who fear Him.

It's good to note that SIN is the root cause to all our calamities. Many would want to justify this as well by asking: What about those criminals who go on sinning and yet they are never being caught by any established authority to bring them to account for their sinful acts. Oh yes! They may continue to escape the trap set out, but it will not last forever. They will one day be called to account for their evil deals either on earth here or when the solemn call to yonder. So, please don't be fooled by those disguise scary looks today and think that they are living better than you.

See the case of Joseph, even when his brothers sold him into slavery. After he has found favor in the sight of his master, Potiphar. His wife wanted to sleep with him because he was very handsome, he refused to do so. For some of us, we would seize that opportunity to gain more favor before Potiphar the master and his wife, which for many will think is a blessing. No. It's not. It's a curse. There are several things, to human beings which will appear as a blessing, but don't get yourself into such reproachable or so-called blessing. It's temporary and the future consequences can be a disaster.

Do you know why most of you struggle with worldly life?

Every time, you say to yourself that this is not good for me to do. Please bear in mind you ought to replace what is seen by God or before men not too good for you to practice via something that is good to put into practice.

Otherwise, you cannot afford to abstain from doing bad things, when there is nothing nearby for you to put into practice, which will serve as a good replacement. You will surely get back to your vomit and lick it for either the second time or over again. So, to save yourself from the challenge of refraining from sin and then, all of the sudden going back to what you once said you cannot do again or no longer interested into it. It is to quickly replace what is evil in your sight with what is good.

Have you ever seen a divorced couple yesterday, after sometimes, those who have gone to court and were pronounced divorce, stealing in disguise to have sexual relationship?

What a shame in disguise? This is why it is good to replace any malpractice with a good one immediately.

This is how I remarried as soon as we were pronounced temporary divorce or separated domicile. In three months interval, I remarried immediately for the fear of not falling into such trap or disgraced lifestyle.

You have to make a decision to be holy in what you do. Nobody can make that decision for you. You have to make it.

The prodigal son and his elder brother with his critic and jealous mindset

Most of us know the story of the prodigal son. Having squandered his resources and realized he has sinned against God and man. However, instead he continually living such life, he chose the possible and favorable contrary — to return to his real father. It's the same with us whenever we faltered and realized it is better to repent than refusing to repent. God is able to restore us to our original stage or even position better than what we were before.

However, once we gained such unmerited favor, let us be also rest assured of the critics or the jealousy of those around us or that will come against us. This has reminded me of President George M. Weah, the underdog president of Liberia, as considered by his critics and those who are jealous that he is not fit to be the president of that nation.

This is how it was when the prodigal son returned home; his father was happy to receive him and even threw out a feast for a once lost son who is now found. Amazing grace!

His elder brother was not happy for the special treatment given to his junior brother whom he considered in his anger expressions to be a vagabond. He lamented that: *"I have been very obedient to you, Papa. Not a single day you have ever thought of treating me like this and now see what you have done for this your so-called son."*

Jealousy has carried many of us into our early graves. You can be walking in the streets thinking that you are alive, but if you don't tame your mindset properly jealousy will either spoil your happiness or end your life in no time.

It's the same with critics. What is seen in political parties across the globe? The losing parties are to dwell in perpetual criticism of the incumbent government until they now reached the throne (seat) of power. What was once seen as others' error will now become their own error.

Sometimes, what the other government was capable of doing before and was criticized, the one currently in power or who just took over power are now incapable to accomplish too.

There are twofold reasons to such stance:

a) Due to pride they can't humble themselves and ask how the previous government did things and acquired such tangible results;
b) Due to shame or reproach they would not be willing to receive from the previous government officials for their lack of know-how.

The above mentioned two scenarios will now lead them to great failure. In fact, they will be worse than the previous one.

For everyone, let's be very careful on how we point accusing fingers, or criticize others lest the ones you once criticized before will be the ones refunding your previous criticism, which sometimes do not help any nation in such impasse we get ourselves into. We will find it difficult to return to our normal state of mind. Criticisms and jealousy have played major role in destroying many of you who have reserved special time for them. I have once lived by criticisms, but it didn't do me any good, but brought enough unbearable rage.

This is something that is very common in several African leadership, the government in power is required to get used to jealousy and fruitless criticisms from the opposition parties whether they like it or not, it will come.

This does not only happen with political parties, even amongst colleagues, the same criticisms and jealousy does exist. This is seen in events where a colleague is been given an unmerited favor. S/He will suffer a great deal of criticism or jealousy. It is killing the social cohesion softly in many organizations across the globe. *You know why? It's because nobody wants the other person better than them.* Nobody has that sense of keeping a low profile when things do not go their way and be willing to give God, the glory for what was given to a colleague, as an unmerited favor (grace), because of jealousy. Let's beware of it.

If you want to increase in any form of wealth, be it Finance, or other Blessings is to find out how everyone is doing it and then do the possible opposite.

Let me explain myself here. I have once been telling people or told people that I will never and ever travel to either Europe or America, if it is not to further my studies, to hustle. I have kept this mindset since 2004 to date. Whatever those friends or relatives who left us in Africa and gone to Europe or America in search of greener pastures, I have actually acquired every other thing they may have missed in Africa.

Do you see that?

Watch out how you carry yourself.
When I was in High School, in the early 1990s I used to hear this proverb from schoolmates or classmates. **"It is not the coat that matters, but the man in the coat."** This was my then mindset, until in early 2000s, where I have lived and worked in a French system. The above-mentioned adage held much importance to me.

One day, in 2007 – to be precise. I told this above clever saying to one of my colleagues, Pascal Sarr, in a French language: ***"l'habile ne fait pas le moine"*** He sharply responded: ***Mais c'est par l'habile qu'on reconnait le moine.*** It is through the clothes of the monk, he is recognized as a monk I paused and continue what I was doing, because with Pascal, he's always having his own way seeing different from everyone. So, I ignored him.

Almost, ten years later, my wife, Rose who was also from Catholic background knows this clever saying. She was being difficult with me in changing my clothing style, but I was not willing to do so. She kept harassing me on daily basis to replace my old clothes from my previous failed marriage. She does not want to see me in those clothing. *"I am not comfortable with any of them."* This pressure continues to mount. One day, in our tense discussion, I expressed to her in a French language so that she can leave me alone: *"l'habile ne fait pas le moine"* She sharply responded: *Mais c'est par l'habile qu'on reconnait le moine.* It was tough with me, but I did process it and reconsidered it to be a candid piece of advice. I have to change my clothing style and look smart instead. She is not saying that I should break a bank in order to look smart, but let start from somewhere. She took ownership of the process. Today, it is history.

Brethren, strive to look very good. It might seem costly, but it is worth the effort.

On a Tuesday early morning, 9th October 2018 I had my 407 Peugeot salon car in the garage for repairs because the vehicle, due to Dakar's poor environment system wherein whenever it rains here, the rainy waters, instead of been absorbed by the soil, it is stationed for several days making non paved roads messy and rendering fragile cars to be stationed to mechanic hospitals for several days. In just a week interval, I have thus far spent a considerable amount of money in taxi fares. Horrible right? Yes. It is very much horrible.

As I stood before the FBN bank waiting for it to open, I tried to clear few pending files. Nowadays, with the advent of technology, you are no longer required to be into cubical before you can carry out your duties. That was then. I hit the WhatsApp I found out that Acting DAF, business cards have run out, and he was requesting a new set of cards. I responded it will be taken care of, and quickly moved on to notify the service provider that usually produce those kind of services to get me the dummies for approval before they are printed and delivered.

I was, one afternoon, contemplating, then, all of the sudden, I thought of something and that was to establish a company where I will not be the one running it, but the technocrats instead. Those who are trained for that as any young novice entrepreneur, I first got overwhelmed and thoughts that weren't in place kept flooding my mind. Stop! I shouted. Comrade! Again, I shouted, it is not like that. Do some research either on the internet to see whether the name you intend to give your organization is not already somebody's company name? If it does, it will surely cost you, you know.

Then, I googled this name: *Dakar by Day*. I have also learnt to question everything. So, I questioned this name also. Why Dakar, why not Freetown, your home city? Not knowing where to begin my argument, I quickly got a change of mind. For the solutions I intend to present, though they will obviously have their origin or debut in Dakar, which will now serve as a pipeline for the rest of Africa, and possibly, for most of our stranded African brothers and sisters who might intend to come back home to do something for their respective motherland(s) or decide to do something for Africa as a whole, not just for their immediate family members, other relatives or friends, but for Africa's general common goal.

Then, the name came to mind, it is called: AFRICA BY DAY. I again, googled this name. All I saw was Africa Day, but never *Africa By Day*. I wanted it to be unique. This is not going to be family startups, though, it may start with an individual, but the main goal is to bring tangible solutions to African issues. Is it going to be easy? Never, God will see me through. Amen.

The Crocodile & the Buffalo

A story is told, which is actually a true story, to be precise is; an incident occurred between the buffalo and the crocodile. The crocodile was on its hunting scene near the river bank or shore, some will put it. Then, the buffalo came also in search of solace – that is, to drink water. Well, the crocodile said to itself that I have got prey to feed on. It positioned itself in that stepping stone mode and as soon as the buffalo drew nearer, it emerged and the buffalo turned to run for its life. It grasped the left foot of the buffalo.

The buffalo has some stand because it could stand on the solid ground to get energy and struggles to pull off its left leg from the mouth of the crocodile. For many of us, as I am writing this story have either gone through similar scenario and today we have broken free from it or will one day, go through it. If at all, we are supposed to go through it.

In one man of God, *Pastor Marcello TUNASI's* books entitled: *45 Strategies against Temptation.* I don't know exactly the correct number of the strategy, but whenever you find yourself in this kind of a mess. Relax, it will not be with you forever. The strategy is called: **_The Strategy of porous or weak fishing net_**. You see whenever you go fishing and you find yourself with either a weak fishing net or porous fishing net, you will not get a good catch of fish. Difficulties in life (and if I should put them in this form: the devil's schemes, which is by far common to many of us), are like that weak fishing net. Just give them some times of effort. You can breakthrough. You do not sit there and do not do anything about it. You do something about it and let the struggle continues, but let it be in a very mild form. The time you least expect your release, will soon show up.

This is how the buffalo used the strategy of the weak or porous fishing net. It didn't fight till, all its power was over, and then, gave up, but bit by bit it struggled and finally, the crocodile keep holding the buffalo's left foot, however, the jaw and teeth of the crocodile got tired too and it gave up the foot of the buffalo and it ran for safety. Though, with the pain in the left foot, but it was better than remaining in the mouth of the crocodile or finally finding itself in the belly of the crocodile.

Have you ever encountered such telling blows in your life? When you are graciously catering to the wellbeing of your children and all you received in return blunt reproaches and insults? If so, may the Almighty God help you go through it successfully. Amen.

My worse life began, when I one day, decided with my then wife, now my ex to bring near us our two daughters: Evon & Jeannesa. Not knowing that I was bringing in trouble for myself instead of a peaceful home. In July 2013, Jeannesa arrived and a month later, then, came in Evon. They met their junior brother who was then registered into an International School of Dakar. What a blunder for me! Jealousy emerged, Evon broke his left foot and he struggled with it for at least three months. He later recovered from that incidence. It was the beginning of our final foreseeing separation commonly called divorce.

The home immediately became a two factions home, wherein mommy with her two recalcitrant daughters and the dad with his god-fearing toddler son. Tensions continued to mount and then, I started relating the message of concern to lovely brethren in our church, in the person of my now ex-pastor, but he never had time for me, however, whenever my now ex called him for any issue between us, he is very available to come and handle that.

This other day I received a message from Jeannesa bullshitting me that I am the worst dad in the whole world. I was the one feeding her, yet she had the audacity to speak to me in that manner. Anyway, like I said to them, time will tell. You will one day reflect on your lives and know that you were very wrong for shunning my pieces of advice.

I am currently paying child support, yet the child I am paying child support for is actually living with me and not with his mom. My son, Ebenezer is with me but Jeannesa, who insulted me and considered me the worse dad was sent to school in Banjul, The Gambia. Unfortunate for her, the same worst father in the entire world is the one who sustained her in her studies. Guess what, now she left Banjul and returned to Dakar near her mom. I kept using the strategy of the weak net where I know they will not remain in school forever. In fact, in the ECOWAS system, as soon as your child hits 24 years of age, he/she is no longer catered for as your dependent. I hope these young girls Jeannesa & Evon, know this. Time will soon help me get out of the crocodile's mouth and leave my foot (my finances) and will be free from any problem from both them and their mom.

My mom objected to my relationship with this woman, but I didn't listen to her, because I was in love. However, it was in fact, a training ground for me today, because I am still learning valuable lessons from all the trauma she caused me from humbled beginning to where I am today. Only now I got to know that if you are unfortunate to get into the hands of a wicked woman as a wife, even her offspring will tend to be very wicked in their dealings. I salute her for that.

No regrets at all, but credible lessons for anyone who sensed this kind of practice in either their relationship to be very cautious on how to handle things. Relax, and diligently fight your battle in a bit by bit way like what the buffalo did. Trouble may last for a night, but joy will surely emerge in the morning.

Transition

I love writing. Yes, I said, I love writing. Anything for everything, I write down notes for my reminders. In church, I write when the pastor preaches. In meetings, I write down notes. Even, if someone insults me, I write down the experience.

This day, 8th May 2017 I went to pick up my Ebenezer from school. Once at their class door, I spotted in his arms, a pizza case and other goodies. From a distance, he said, help me carry these ones so that I can carry my school bag. I opted for his school bag instead and let him take care of his goods his mom (who is now my ex) has brought to him at the school.

I have observed, every time, she comes to his school with things, there is change in attitude in the life of my son.   Change here, I meant, negative behaviors from his part, which was also having a side effect in my new home with now wife, Rose.

Rose, by nature, is an uncontrollable extrovert. She will never tell you later, but will hit back instantly like an instant Nescafe. I have trouble in handling this behavior. She speaks out her piece of mind and later on, she regrets and asks for forgiveness. And, because it has become too much for her, she sometimes, refrained from asking for forgiveness, because she is now ashamed of reminding her that I told you not to respond instantly whenever an issue popped up. However, you are yet to learn this.

I came home, trying to cope with the issues of the day, bang! My wife, Rose, as she was dishing out the food on the table for us all to eat, I don't know what Ebenezer did, she responded: *I am now going to show you that, I am not your real mom*. I held my front head with my right palm and gently said to here, "stop". She could not hold it, but burst into explanation.

Ebenezer arrived with his pizza and other food stuffs that his mom has brought to school and he waited for his junior brother, Tresor to come and they can ate together. You could see them celebrating. After they have eaten enough and even left some. They moved in their room, and there, Ebenezer said that I am a wicked woman (in French: *Je suis mechante*). 'I will henceforth treat him like I am not his real mother. No wonder, step mothers tend to treat step children very bad, because no matter what you do, they will never recognize your goodness to them." She grudging ended her speech.

The sweetest soup dish, she then prepared and we were eating, became very tasteless in my mouth. Fortunately for me, I had been listening to an audiobook *Transition*, which spelt out these challenges couples faced in either their first, second, third or at most, fourth marriages. Yet, I was really disturbed. This is my own side of transition. I have to grow mature and at least, one day, I can share it with people either within my environment or across the world, as a testimony that the good Lord God, has brought me through, successfully. So, never mind, whether you are currently going through it now, or it is about to happen to you, take courage. It is surmountable. I am here and I have been there, survived it and you can overcome it too.

After, we have finished eating, I asked the children to go out of the kitchen where it is designated as our dining room, and asked her to slightly close the kitchen door behind us. I told her, Rose, my baby I love you plenty. And this, you know it very well, right? She answered, yes. Then, after the jingo, I went on and told her to treat Ebenezer, as her REAL son. Give him the discipline that you see fit, it is for his own good. Besides, if you treat him well, obviously, the world will see it even if he does not recognize it. The Most High God will surely reward you for that. However, please be careful, not to let emotions take the better side of your life, which will end in regrets.

Many women have done so and when the harvest was ready for them, it is rather the shame, which was present for them to harvest.   So, please don't give the devil a foothold in your self—esteemed and noble wife as it is stipulated in the book of Proverbs 31 starting from verses 10 through 31.

After having gone through discussing this with her, I requested that Ebenezer too, come in for me to discuss with him. Ebenezer arrived and asked him to kneel down and face some questionings.

Me: Why do you tell maman that she is a wicked woman?

Eben: No papa, it is not me that said that. It is Tresor that said it.

Me. I restructured my question for his better understanding. "Ebenezer," I said. "You know me, right?"

Eben: Yes papa.

Me: Why do you tell maman that she is a wicked woman?

Eben: Again, it is not me that said that, papa.

It is rather a question I asked and he responded, "Is maman a wicked woman?"

To this, infront of my angry wife, I said, "there is a problem. He does not seem to tell me the truth. So, let Tresor come in here."

Me: Tresor, Why do you tell maman that she is a wicked woman?

Tresor: No, papa. It is Ebenezer that asked me the question, and then, I answered him, you just want me to say that it is maman that is a wicked woman, right? So I came and told maman that Ebenezer is saying, you are a wicked woman.

Me: I again asked Treson, why do you tell maman that she is a wicked woman?

Tresor: No, papa. It is Ebenezer that said that and not me.

I have told my children that if you tell me the truth. Even if you were supposed to receive a beating, I prevent that one from happening, because I want you to learn to say only the truth and nothing else. So, I did that rehearsal for Tresor, my bonus son. I love him so much for his extrovert stance and fearless mindset. However, there is one element I need to chip off his life, is lying.

This is a boy, whose biological father on a phone discussion at Gbessia Airport in Conakry, told me I am handing this boy to you, as your son. For that reason, I considered him as my legal son. Unfortunately, this does not happen, because there is a difference between verbal handover and written or official handing over. When it was time for this paper work to be done, I received partial adoption instead and never complete adoption. To which, my office, BACOCO rejected the entire process altogether. So he is rather considered as my step—son and never my real for there is NO PROOF to that to date.

So after having gone through the rehearsal with him (Tresor)

Me: I again said to Tresor. I am going to pose this same question, but in different form for at least, four times: "Who said that maman is a wicked woman?"

To the above-mentioned question, Tresor responded: "It is me."

I kept quiet for a while and told to stand up and go to the parlor. He is free from any trouble from side, however, I told him, and he should stop lying. Or, if he does lie, as soon as it is noticed and we asked him, let him say the truth. Next time, if he does and does not respond immediately, we will discipline him for that constant faux pas.

Me: Ebenezer why do you ask this probing question to Tresor?

Eben: Nothing.

Me: You are Tresor's elder brother. Never again you ask him such question. Because of your unscrupulous probing question, I will beat you not to ever again pose such question in this house.

I gave Ebenezer, two beats only, his step-mom stepped in to part us because she saw it too much for him as a child to bear such a strong beating. To her intervention, I recognized that she loves him a lot, but was also filled with a jealous stance like me too when I spotted the pizza case in school with Ebenezer. So, she was angry for that, but like all human beings. We get angry and those around us do not know what the origin of the anger is in the first place. It requires an in-depth investigations or strong probing with courage to actually see where lies the problem at stake.

Later that night, I asked my wife, Rose whether she was angry when Ebenezer arrived with those items. No! She exclaimed. Why would I be angry for that? It is her son, there is no need for me to get angry. Were you not taking things to school for Ebenezer, when he was with the mum? I responded, "Yes". Yet, I continued by telling her that, "as for me, let me not pretend, I was angry". However, thank God for some of the lessons I have thus far learnt from many audiobooks that spoke to me about divorce scenes. In them, I have discovered a lot of lessons.

"You will continue to suffer if you have an emotional reaction to everything that is said to you. True power is

sitting back and observing everything with logic. If words control you that means everyone else can control you, Breath and allow things to pass."
*** Bruce Lee ***

Conclusion

Why I fail is a success metaphor in a negative form. A book, which will provide you real, but slight edge life stories, which have led you to few failures in your personal life unknown to you and also few successes in the same rhythm. My two sons always asked me this question: What do you mean whenever you say, "That's how life is". The only challenge now is this. Now that you can identify what has led to your previous failure(s), why not allow that experience to serve as a pipeline minister to see you through future challenges.

www.ingramcontent.com/pod-product-compliance
Lightning Source LLC
Chambersburg PA
CBHW022128050726
47590CB00002B/461